DevOps in Python

Infrastructure as Python

Second Edition

Moshe Zadka

Apress®

DevOps in Python: Infrastructure as Python

Moshe Zadka
Belmont, CA, USA

ISBN-13 (pbk): 978-1-4842-7995-3
https://doi.org/10.1007/978-1-4842-7996-0

ISBN-13 (electronic): 978-1-4842-7996-0

Managing Director, Apress Media LLC: Welmoed Spahr
Acquisitions Editor: Celestin Suresh John
Development Editor: James Markham
Coordinating Editor: Divya Modi
Copy Editor: Kim Burton

Cover designed by eStudioCalamar

Cover image designed by Pixabay

Distributed to the book trade worldwide by Springer Science+Business Media New York, 1 New York Plaza, Suite 4600, New York, NY 10004-1562, USA. Phone 1-800-SPRINGER, fax (201) 348-4505, e-mail orders-ny@springer-sbm.com, or visit www.springeronline.com. Apress Media, LLC is a California LLC and the sole member (owner) is Springer Science + Business Media Finance Inc (SSBM Finance Inc). SSBM Finance Inc is a **Delaware** corporation.

For information on translations, please e-mail booktranslations@springernature.com; for reprint, paperback, or audio rights, please e-mail bookpermissions@springernature.com.

Apress titles may be purchased in bulk for academic, corporate, or promotional use. eBook versions and licenses are also available for most titles. For more information, reference our Print and eBook Bulk Sales web page at http://www.apress.com/bulk-sales.

Any source code or other supplementary material referenced by the author in this book is available to readers on GitHub (github.com/apress). For more detailed information, please visit http://www.apress.com; https://github.com/Apress/DevOps-in-Python-2nd-ed-

Printed on acid-free paper

Dedicated to A and N, my favorite two projects

Table of Contents

About the Author

 **Moshe Zadka** has been involved in the Linux community since 1998, helping in Linux "installation parties." He has been programming Python since 1999 and has contributed to the core Python interpreter. Moshe has been a DevOps/SRE since before those terms existed, caring deeply about software reliability, build reproducibility, and more. He has worked in companies as small as three people and as big as tens of thousands—and usually in a position where software meets system administration.

About the Technical Reviewer

 **Martyn Bristow** is a software developer in the United Kingdom. He began using Python as a researcher but is now an experienced broad user of Python for data analysis, software test automation, and DevOps. He currently builds data analysis web apps in Python deployed to Kubernetes.

You can find Martyn on GitHub @martynbristow.

Acknowledgments

Thanks to my wife, Jennifer Zadka, without whose support I could not have written this book.

Thanks to my parents, Yaacov and Pnina Zadka, who taught me how to learn.

Thanks to my advisor, Yael Karshon, who taught me how to write.

Thanks to Mahmoud Hashemi for inspiration and encouragement.

Thanks to Mark Williams for being there for me.

Thanks to Glyph Lefkowitz for teaching me about Python, programming, and being a good person.

Thanks to Brennon Church and Andrea Ross, who supported my personal growth and learning journey.

Introduction

Python began as a language to automate an operating system: the Amoeba. A typical Unix shell would be ill-suited since it had an API, not just textual file representations. The Amoeba OS is a relic now. However, Python continues to be a useful tool for automation of operations—the heart of typical DevOps work.

It is easy to learn and easy to write readable code is a necessity when a critical part of the work is responding to a 4 a.m. alert and modifying some misbehaving program.

It has powerful bindings to C and C++, the universal languages of the operating system—and yet is natively memory-safe, leading to few crashes at the automation layer.

Finally, although not true when it was created, Python is one of the most popular languages. This means that it is relatively easy to hire people with Python experience and easy to get training materials and courses for people who need to learn on the job.

This book guides you through how to take advantage of Python to automate operations.

To get the most out of the book, you need to be somewhat familiar with Python. If you are new to Python, there are many great resources to learn it, including the official Python tutorial at docs.python.org. You also need to be somewhat familiar with Unix-like operating systems like Linux, especially how to use the command line.

CHAPTER 1

Installing Python

Before you can use Python, you need to install it. Some operating systems, such as macOS and some Linux variants, have Python preinstalled. Those versions of Python, colloquially called system Python, often make poor defaults for people who want to develop in Python.

The version of Python installed is often behind the latest practices. System integrators often patch Python in ways that can lead to surprises. For example, Debian-based Python is often missing modules like venv and ensurepip. macOS Python links against a Mac shim around its native SSL library. Those things mean, especially when starting and consuming FAQs and web resources, it is better to install Python from scratch.

This chapter covers a few ways to do so and the pros and cons of each.

1.1 OS Packages

Volunteers have built ready-to-install packages for some of the more popular operating systems.

The most famous is the deadsnakes PPA (Personal Package Archives). The dead in the name refers to the fact that those packages are already built—with the metaphor that sources are "alive." Those packages are built for Ubuntu and usually support all the versions of Ubuntu that are still supported upstream. Getting those packages is done with a simple

```
$ sudo add-apt-repository ppa:deadsnakes/ppa
$ sudo apt update
```

© Moshe Zadka 2022
M. Zadka, *DevOps in Python*, https://doi.org/10.1007/978-1-4842-7996-0_1

On macOS, the Homebrew third-party package manager has up-to-date Python packages. An introduction to Homebrew is beyond the scope of this book. Homebrew being a rolling release, the Python version is upgraded from time to time. While this means that it is a useful way to get an up-to-date Python, it makes it a poor target for reliably distributing tools.

It also has some downsides for doing day-to-day development. Since it upgrades quickly after a new Python release, development environments can break quickly and without warning. It also means that sometimes code can stop working; even if you are careful to watch upcoming Python versions for breaking changes, not all packages will. Homebrew is a good fit when needing a well-built up-to-date Python interpreter for a one-off task. Writing a quick script to analyze data, or automate some APIs, is a good use of Homebrew Python.

Finally, for Windows, it is possible to download an installer from Python.org for any version of Python.

1.2 Using pyenv

pyenv tends to offer the highest return on investment for installing Python for local development. The initial setup does have some subtleties. However, it allows installing many side-by-side Python versions as needed. It also allows you to manage how each is accessed—either using a per-user default or a per-directory default.

Installing pyenv itself depends on the operating system. On a macOS, the easiest way is to install it via Homebrew. Note that in this case, pyenv itself might need to be upgraded to install new versions of Python.

On a Unix-based operating system, such as Linux or FreeBSD, the easiest way to install pyenv is by using the `curl|bash` command.

```
$ PROJECT=https://github.com/pyenv/pyenv-installer \
  PATH=raw/master/bin/pyenv-installer \
  curl -L $PROJECT/PATH | bash
```

Of course, this comes with its own security issues and could be replaced with a two-step process where you can inspect the shell script before running or even use git-checkout to pin to a specific revision.

```
$ git clone https://github.com/pyenv/pyenv-installer
```

```
$ cd pyenv-installer
$ bash pyenv-installer
```

Unfortunately, pyenv does not work on Windows.

After installing pyenv, it is useful to integrate it with the running shell. You do this by adding the following to the shell initialization file (e.g., .bash_profile).

```
export PATH="~/.pyenv/bin:$PATH"
eval "$(pyenv init -)"
eval "$(pyenv virtualenv-init -)"
```

This allows pyenv to properly intercept all the necessary commands.

pyenv separates the notion of *installed* interpreters from *available* interpreters. Enter the following to install a version.

```
$ pyenv install <version>
```

For CPython, <version> is the version number, such as 3.6.6 or 3.7.0rc1.

An *installed* version is distinct from an available version. Versions are available globally (for a user) by using

```
$ pyenv global 3.7.0
```

or locally by using

```
$ pyenv local 3.7.0
```

Local means they are available in a given directory. This is done by putting a python-version.txt file in this directory. This is important for version-controlled repositories, but a few different strategies are used to manage those. One strategy is to add this file to the ignored list. This is useful for heterogeneous teams or open source projects. Another strategy is to check in the file so that the same version of Python is used in the repository.

Note that since pyenv is designed to install side-by-side versions of Python, it has no concept of upgrading Python. A newer Python version needs to be installed with pyenv and then set as the default.

By default, pyenv installs non-optimized versions of Python. If optimized versions are needed, enter the following.

```
env PYTHON_CONFIGURE_OPTS="--enable-shared
                           --enable-optimizations
```

```
                      --with-computed-gotos
                      --with-lto
                      --enable-ipv6" pyenv install
```

Let's build a version that is pretty similar to binary versions from python.org.

1.3 Building Python from Source

The main challenge in building Python from source is that, in some sense, it is too forgiving. It is all too easy to build it with one of the built-in modules disabled because its dependency was not detected. This is why it is important to know which dependencies are fragile and how to make sure a local installation is good.

The first fragile dependency is SSL. It is disabled by default and must be enabled in Modules/Setup.dist. Carefully follow the instructions there about the location of the OpenSSL library. If you have installed OpenSSL via system packages, it is usually in /usr/. If you have installed it from source, it is usually in /usr/local.

The most important thing is to know how to test for it. When Python is done building, run ./python.exe -c 'import _ssl'. That .exe is not a mistake; this is how the build process calls the newly built executable, which is renamed to Python during installation. If this succeeds, the SSL module was built correctly.

Another extension that can fail to build is SQLite. Since it is a built-in, many third-party packages depend on it, even if you are not using it yourself. This means a Python installation without the SQLite module is pretty broken. Test it by running ./python.exe -c 'import sqlite3'.

In a Debian-based system (such as Ubuntu), libsqlite3-dev is required for this to succeed. In a Red Hat-based system (such as Fedora or CentOS), libsqlite3-dev is required for this to succeed.

Next, check for _ctypes with ./python.exe -c 'import _ctypes'. If this fails, likely, the libffi headers are not installed.

Finally, remember to run the built-in regression test suite after building from source. This ensures that there have been no silly mistakes while building the package.

1.4 PyPy

The usual implementation of Python is sometimes known as CPython to distinguish it from the language proper. The most popular alternative implementation is PyPy, a Python-based JIT implementation of Python in Python. Because it has a dynamic JIT (just-in-time) compilation to assembly, it can sometimes achieve phenomenal speed-ups (three times or even ten times) over regular Python.

There are sometimes challenges in using PyPy. Many tools and packages are tested only with CPython. However, sometimes spending the effort to check if PyPy is compatible with the environment is worth it if performance matters.

There are a few subtleties in installing Python from source. While it is theoretically possible to translate using CPython, in practice, the optimizations in PyPy mean that translating using PyPy works on more reasonable machines. Even when installing from source, it is better to first install a binary version to bootstrap.

The bootstrapping version should be PyPy, not PyPy3. PyPy is written in the Python 2 dialect, which is one of the only cases where worrying about the deprecation is irrelevant since PyPy is a Python 2 dialect interpreter. PyPy3 is the Python 3 dialect implementation, which is usually better in production as most packages are slowly dropping support for Python 2.

The latest PyPy3 supports 3.5 features of Python, as well as f-strings. However, the latest async features, added in Python 3.6, do not work.

1.5 Anaconda

The closest to a system Python that is still reasonable for use as a development platform is Anaconda, a *metadistribution*. It is, in essence, an operating system on top of the operating system. Anaconda has its grounding in the scientific computing community, and so its Python comes with easy-to-install modules for many scientific applications. Many of these modules are non-trivial to install from PyPI, requiring a complicated build environment.

It is possible to install multiple Anaconda environments on the same machine. This is handy when needing different Python versions or different versions of PyPI modules.

To bootstrap Anaconda, you can use the bash installer available at `https://conda.io/miniconda.html`. The installer also modifies `~/.bash_profile` to add the path to conda, the installer.

conda environments are created using `conda create --name <name>` and activated using `source conda activate <name>`. There is no easy way to use inactivated environments. It is possible to create a conda environment while installing packages: `conda create --name some-name python`. You can specify the version using = – `conda create --name some-name python=3.5`. It is also possible to install more packages into a conda environment, using `conda install package[=version]`, after the environment has been activated. Anaconda has a lot of prebuilt Python packages, especially ones that are non-trivial to build locally. This makes it a good choice if those packages are important to your use case.

1.6 Summary

Running a Python program requires an interpreter installed on the system. Depending on the operating system and the versions, there are several different ways to install Python. Using the system Python is a problematic option. On macOS and Unix systems, using pyenv is almost always the preferred option. On Windows, using the prepackaged installers from Python.org is often a good idea.

CHAPTER 2

Packaging

One of the main strengths of Python is the *ecosystem*, the third-party packages on PyPI. There are packages to do anything from running computations in parallel on GPUs for machine learning to reducing the boilerplate needed for writing classes. This means that a lot of the practical work with Python is handling the third-party dependencies.

The current packaging tooling is pretty good, but things have not always been this way. It is important to understand which best practices are antiquated rituals based on faulty assumptions but have some merit and are actually good ideas.

When dealing with packaging, there are two ways to interact. One is to be a consumer wanting to use the functionality of a package. Another is to be the producer, publishing a package. These describe, usually, different development tasks, not different people.

It is important to have a solid understanding of the consumer side of packages before moving to production. If the goal of a package publisher is to be useful to the package user, it is crucial to imagine the last mile before starting to write a single line of code.

2.1 Virtual Environments

Virtual environments are often misunderstood because the concept of environments is not clear. A Python environment refers to the root of the Python installation. The reason an environment is important is because of the `lib/site-packages` subdirectory of that root. The `lib/site-packages` subdirectory is where third-party packages are installed.

The most popular tool to *add* packages to an environment is `pip`, which is covered in the next section. Before using `pip`, it is important to understand how virtual environments work.

A real environment is based on Python installation, which means that to get a new real environment, a new Python must be installed and often rebuilt. This is sometimes an expensive proposition.

© Moshe Zadka 2022

M. Zadka, *DevOps in Python*, https://doi.org/10.1007/978-1-4842-7996-0_2

The advantage of a *virtual* environment is that it is cheap to set up and tear down. Some modern Python tooling takes advantage of that, setting up and tearing down virtual environments as a normal part of their operation. Setting up and tearing down virtual environments, being cheap and fast, is also a common part of Python developer workflow.

A virtual environment copies the minimum necessary out of the real environment to mislead Python into thinking it has a new root. The precise file structure is less important than remembering that the command to create a virtual environment is simple and fast.

Here, *simple* means that all the command does is copy some files and perhaps make a few symbolic links. Because of that, there are a few failure modes—mostly when file creation fails because of permission issues or a full disk.

There are two ways to use virtual environments: activated and inactivated. To use an inactivated virtual environment, which is most common in scripts and automated procedures, you explicitly call Python from the virtual environment.

This means that a virtual environment in /home/name/venvs/my-special-env calling /home/name/venvs/my-special-env/bin/python has a Python process that uses this environment. For example, /home/name/venvs/my-special-env/bin/python -m pip runs pip but installs in the virtual environment.

Note that entrypoint-based scripts are installed alongside Python, so running /home/name/venvs/my-special-env/bin/pip also installs packages in the virtual environment.

The other way to use a virtual environment is to activate it. Activating a virtual environment in a bash-like shell means *sourcing* its activated script.

```
$ source /home/name/venvs/my-special-env/bin/activate
```

The sourcing sets a few environment variables, only one of which is important. The important variable is PATH, which gets prefixed by /home/name/venvs/my-special-env/bin. This means that commands like python or pip are found there first. Two cosmetic variables are set. $VIRTUAL_ENV points to the root of the environment. This is useful in management scripts that want to be aware of virtual environments. PS1 is prefixed with (my-special-env), which is useful for visualizing the virtual environment while working interactively in the console.

It is generally a good practice to only install third-party packages inside a virtual environment. Combined with the fact that virtual environments are cheap, if one gets into a bad state, it is best to remove the whole directory and start from scratch.

For example, imagine a bad package install that causes the Python start-up to fail. Even running `pip uninstall` is impossible since `pip` fails on start-up. However, the cheapness means you can remove the whole virtual environment and re-create it with a good set of packages.

A modern practice is to move increasingly toward treating virtual environments as semi-immutable. After creating them, there is a single stage for installing all required packages. Instead of modifying the virtual environment if an upgrade is required, destroy the environment, re-create, and reinstall.

The modern way to create virtual environments is to use the venv standard library module. This only works on Python 3. Since Python 2 has been strongly deprecated since the beginning of 2020, it is best avoided in any case.

venv is used as a command with `python -m venv <directory>`, as there is no dedicated `entrypoint`. It creates the directory for the environment.

It is best if this directory does not exist before that. A best practice is to remove it before creating the environment. There are also two options for creating the environment: which interpreter to use and what initial packages to install.

2.2 pip

The packaging tool for Python is `pip`. There have been other tools that have mostly been abandoned by the community and should not be used.

Installations of Python used to not come with `pip` out of the box. This has changed in recent versions, but many versions which are still supported do not have it. When running on such a version, `python -m ensurepip` installs it.

Some Python installations, especially system ones, disable `ensurepip`. When lacking `ensurepip`, there is a way of manually getting it: `get-pip.py`. This is a single downloadable file that, when executed, unpacks `pip`.

Luckily, `pip` is the only package that needs these weird gyrations to install. All other packages can, and should, be installed using `pip`.

For example, if `sample-environment` is a virtual environment, installing the `glom` package can be done with the following code.

```
$ ./sample-environment/bin/python -m pip install glom
...
$ ./sample-environment/bin/python -m glom
{}
```

The last command tests that `glom` has been properly installed. Glom is a package to handle deeply-nested data, and called with no arguments, outputs an empty Python dictionary. This makes it handy for quickly testing whether a new virtual environment can install new packages properly.

Internally, `pip` is also treated as a third-party package. Upgrading `pip` itself is done with `pip install --upgrade pip`.

Depending on how Python was installed, its real environment might or might not be modifiable by the user. Many instructions in various README files and blogs might encourage using `sudo pip install`. This is almost always the wrong thing to do; it installs the packages in the global environment.

The `pip install` command downloads and installs all dependencies. However, it can fail to downgrade incompatible packages. It is always possible to install explicit versions: `pip install package-name==<version>` installs this precise version. This is also a good way for local testing to get explicitly non-general-availability packages, such as release candidates, beta, or similar.

If `wheel` is installed, `pip` builds, and usually caches, wheels for packages. This is especially useful when dealing with a high virtual environment churn since installing a cached wheel is a fast operation. This is also highly useful when dealing with native or binary packages that need to be compiled with a C compiler. A wheel cache eliminates the need to build it again.

`pip` does allow uninstalling with `pip uninstall <package>`. This command, by default, requires manual confirmation. Except for exotic circumstances, this command is not used. If an unintended package has snuck in, the usual response is to destroy the environment and rebuild it. For similar reasons, `pip install --upgrade <package>` is not often needed; the common response is to destroy and re-create the environment. There is one situation where it is a good idea.

`pip install` supports a requirements file: `pip install --requirements` or `pip install -r`. The requirements file simply has one package per line. This is no different from specifying packages on the command line. However, requirement files often specify strict dependencies. A requirements file can be *generated* from an environment with `pip freeze`.

Like most individual packages or wheels, installing anything that is not strict and closed under requirements requires `pip` to decide which dependencies to install. The general problem of dependency resolution does not have an efficient and complete solution. Different strategies are possible to approach such a solution.

The way pip resolves dependencies is by using *backtracking*. This means that it optimistically tries to download the latest possible requirements recursively. If a dependency conflict is found, it backtracks; try a different option.

As an example, consider three packages.

- top

- middle

- base

There are two base versions: 1.0 and 2.0. The package dependencies are setup. cfg files.

The following is for the top.

```
[metadata]
name = top
version = 1.0
[options]
install_requires =
    base
    middle
```

The following is for the middle.

```
[metadata]
name = middle
version = 1.0
[options]
install_requires =
    base<2.0
```

The base package has two versions: 1.0 and 2.0. It does not have any dependencies.

Because top depends directly on base, pre-backtracking versions of pip get the latest and then have a failed resolution.

```
$ pip install top
Looking in links: .
Collecting top
Collecting middle (from top)
```

```
Collecting base (from top)
middle 1.0 has requirement base<2.0, but you'll have base 2.0 which is
incompatible.
Installing collected packages: base, middle, top
Successfully installed base-2.0 middle-1.0 top-1.0
```

The backtracking algorithm discards the base 2.0 version.

```
$ pip install top
Looking in links: .
Processing ./top-1.0-py3-none-any.whl
Processing ./base-2.0-py3-none-any.whl
Processing ./middle-1.0-py3-none-any.whl
Processing ./base-1.0-py3-none-any.whl
Installing collected packages: base, middle, top
Successfully installed base-1.0 middle-1.0 top-1.0
```

This solution has the advantage that it is *complete*, but it can take unfeasible amounts of time in certain cases. This is rare, but merely taking a *long* time is not.

One way to increase the speed is to include >= dependencies in the loose requirements. This is usually a good idea since packages are better at guaranteeing backward compatibility than forward compatibility. As a side benefit, this can dramatically reduce the solution space that pip needs to backtrack in.

In most scenarios, it is better to use strict requirements for day-to-day development and regenerate the strict requirements from the loose requirements (which can take a while) on a cadence that balances keeping up to date with churn.

2.3 Setup and Wheels

The term *third party* (as in third-party packages) refers to someone other than the Python core developers (first-party) or the local developers (second-party). I have covered how to install first-party packages in the installation section. You used pip and virtualenv to install third-party packages. It is time to finally turn your attention to the missing link: local development and installing local packages or second-party packages.

Note that the word *package* here means something different from post-installation. In Python, a package is an importable directory, a way to keep multiple modules together. The pedantic way to call installable things is *distribution*. A distribution can correspond to no packages (it can be a top-level single-module distribution) or multiple packages.

It is good to keep a 1-1-1 relationship when packaging things: a single distribution corresponding to one package and named the same. Even if there is only one file, put it as an __init__.py file under a directory.

Packaging is an area that has seen a lot of changes. Copying and pasting from existing packages is not a good idea; good packages are, for the most part, mature packages. Following the latest best practices means making changes to an existing working process.

Starting with setuptools version 61.0.0, it is possible to create a package with only two files besides the code files.

- pyproject.toml

- README.rst

The README is not strictly necessary. However, most source code management systems display it rendered, so it is best to break it out into its own file.

Even an empty pyproject.toml generates a package. However, almost all packages need at least a few more details.

The build-system is the one mandatory section in a non-empty pyproject.toml file. It is usually the first.

```
[build-system]
requires = [
    "setuptools"
]
build-backend = "setuptools.build_meta"
```

Many systems can be used to build valid distributions. The setuptools system, which used to be the only possibility, is now one of several. However, it is still the most popular one.

Most of the rest of the data can be found in the project section.

```
[project]
name = "awesome_package"
version = "0.0.3"
description = "A pretty awesome package"
```

```
readme = "README.rst"
authors = [{name = "My Name",
            email = "me@example.com"}]
dependencies = ["httpx"]
```

For most popular code organizations, this is enough for the setuptools systems to find the code and create a correct package.

There are ways to have setuptools treat the version as dynamic and take it from a file or an attribute. An alternative is to take advantage of pyproject.toml in a structured format and manipulate it directly.

For example, the following code uses a CalVer (calendar versioning) scheme of YEAR.MONTH.release in a month. It uses the built-in zoneinfo module, which requires Python 3.9 or above, and the tomlkit library, which supports roundtrip-preserving TOML parsing and serialization.

```
import tomlkit
import datetime
import os
import pathlib
import zoneinfo

now = datetime.datetime.now(tz=zoneinfo.ZoneInfo("UTC"))
prefix=f"{now.year}.{now.month}."
pyproject = pathlib.Path("pyproject.toml")
data = tomlkit.loads(pyproject.read_text())
current = data["project"].get("version", "")
if current.startswith(prefix):
    serial = int(current.split(".")[-1]) + 1
else:
    serial = 0
version = prefix + str(serial)
data["project"]["version"] = version
pyproject.write_text(tomlkit.dumps(data))
```

Some utilities keep the version synchronized between several files; for example, pyproject.toml and example_package/__init__.py. The best way to use these utilities is by not needing to do it.

If example_package/__init__.py wants to expose the version number, the best way is to calculate it using importlib.metadata.

```
# example_package/__init__.py
from importlib import metada
__version__ = metadata.distribution("example_package").version
del metadata # Keep top-level namespace clean
```

This avoids needing to keep more than one place in sync.

The field dependencies in pyproject.toml is present on almost every package. This is how to mark other distributions that the code needs. It is a good practice to put loose dependencies in pyproject.toml. This is in contrast to exact dependencies, which specify a specific version. A loose dependency looks like Twisted>=17.5, specifying a minimum version but no maximum. Exact dependencies, like Twisted==18.1, are usually a bad idea in pyproject. toml. They should only be used in rare cases, for example, when using significant chunks of a *private* API package.

The pyproject.toml file also allows defining entrypoints. Some frameworks, like Pyramid, allow using entrypoints to add plugin-like features.

It also allows you to define scripts. These used to be console_scripts entrypoints but now have their own section.

```
[project.scripts]
example-command = "example_package.commands:main"
```

The syntax is package.....module:function. This function is called with no arguments when the script is being run.

Usually, this includes command-line parsing, but the following is a short example.

```
# example_package/commands.py
def main():
    print("an example")
```

In this example, running example-command causes the string to print.

```
$ example-command
an example
```

You can build a distribution with `pyproject.toml`, a README.rst, and some Python code. There are several formats a distribution can take, but the one covered here is the *wheel*.

After installing `build` using `pip install build`, run

```
python -m build --wheel
```

This creates a wheel under `dist`. If the wheel needs to be in a different directory, add `--outdir <output directory>` to the command.

You can do several things with the wheel, but it is important to note that one thing you can do is `pip install <wheel file>`. Doing this as part of continuous integration makes sure the wheel, as built by the current directory, is functional.

It is possible to use `python -m build` to create a source distribution. This is usually a good idea to accommodate use cases that prefer to install from source. These use cases are esoteric, but generating the source distribution is easy enough to be worth it.

```
$ python -m build --sdist
```

It is possible to combine the `--sdist` and `--wheel` arguments into one run of `python -m build`. This is also what `python -m build` does by default: create both a source distribution and a wheel.

By default, `python -m build` installs any packages it needs to build the package in a fresh virtual environment. When running `python -m build` in a tight edit-debug loop, perhaps to debug a `setup.cfg`, this can get tedious. In those cases, create and activate a virtual environment, and then run

```
$ python -m build --no-isolation
```

This installs its dependencies in the current environment. While this is not a good fit for production use, this is a faster way to debug packaging issues.

2.4 Binary Wheels

Python is well known and often used as an integration language. One of the ways this integration happens is by linking to native code.

This is usually done using the C Application Binary Interface (C ABI). The C ABI is used not only for integrating with C libraries but with other languages, such as C++, Rust, or Swift, which can generate C ABI-compatible interfaces.

There needs to be some glue code bridging the C ABI to Python to integrate Python with such code. It is possible to write this code by hand.

This is a tedious and error-prone process, so code generators are often used. Cython is a popular generator that uses a Python-compatible language. Although Cython is often used to interface to C ABI libraries, it can be used to generate extensions without such integration. This makes examples slightly simpler, so the following Cython code is used as a running example.

```
#cython: language_level=3

def add(x, y):
    return x + y
```

This code is in the binary_module.pyx file. It is short and does just enough to be clear if it works correctly.

To build code with native integration, the files that describe the build are slightly more complicated.

The pyproject.toml file is no longer empty. It now has two lines.

```
[build-system]
requires = ["setuptools", "cython"]
```

This makes sure the cython package is installed before trying to build a wheel.

The setup.py is no longer minimal. It contains enough code to integrate with Cython.

```
import setuptools
from Cython import Build

setuptools.setup(
    ext_modules=Build.cythonize("binary module.pyx"),
)
```

The Cython.Build.cythonize function does two things.

- Creates (or re-creates) binary_module.c from binary_module.pyx.

- Returns an Extension object.

Since `*.pyx` files are not included by default, it needs to be enabled explicitly in the `MANIFEST.in` file.

```
include *.pyx
```

Since, in this example, there are no regular Python files, the `setup.cfg` does not need to specify any.

```
[metadata]
name = binary_example
version = 1.0
```

With these files, running `python -m build --wheel` builds a binary wheel in `dist` named something like `binary_example-1.0-cp39-cp39-linux_x86_64.whl`. Details of the name depend on the platform, the architecture, and the Python version.

After installing this wheel, it can be used as follows.

```
$ pip install dist/binary_example*.whl
$ python -c 'import binary_module;print(binary_module.add(1, 2))'
3
```

This is a simple example that demonstrates the mechanics of binary packaging. It is designed to show how all the pieces fit together in a small example.

Realistic binary packages are usually more complicated, implementing subtle algorithms that can take advantage of the optimizations Cython gives or wrapping a native-code library.

2.5 manylinux Wheels

A binary wheel is not a pure Python wheel because at least one of its files contains native code. On a Linux system, this native code is a *shared library*, a file with the `.so` suffix for a shared object.

This shared library *links against* other libraries. For a library designed to wrap a specific native library, as with `pygtk` wrapping `gtk`, it links with the wrapped library.

In almost all cases, whether it is designed to wrap a specific library or not, it links against the *standard C library*. This is the library that has C functions like `printf`. Few things can be done in native code without linking against it.

On most modern Linux systems, this linking is usually *dynamic*. This means that the binary wheel does not contain the library it is linked with; it expects to load it at runtime.

If a wheel is built on a different system than the one it is installed on, a library that is *binary compatible* with the one it is linked with has to be installed on the system. If a binary compatible library is not installed, this leads to a failure at import time.

2.5.1 Self-Contained Wheels

The `auditwheel` tool takes binary wheels and patches them to make them more portable. One of its functions is to grab the pieces from dynamic libraries and put them in the wheel. This allows the wheels to be installed without requiring a different library.

For `auditwheel` to work correctly, the `patchelf` utility needs to be installed. Older versions might produce wheels that break in strange ways. The safest way to have the right version of `patchelf` is to download the latest source distribution and build it.

To make a self-contained wheel, first, build a regular build. This might require careful reading of the instructions for building the package from source. This results in the regular binary wheel in `dist/`. This was the case in the example before with the `binary_example` module.

After this is done, run

```
$ auditwheel repair --plat linux_x86_64 dist/*.whl
```

By default, `auditwheel` creates the self-contained wheel in a `wheelhouse` subdirectory. The wheel created is self-contained but expects to be installed on a compatible version of Linux.

2.5.2 Portable Wheels

The `--plat` flag in `auditwheel` is the platform tag. If it is `linux_<cpu architecture>`, the wheel makes no guarantees about which GNU C Library it is compatible with.

Wheels like that should only be installed on a compatible Linux system. To avoid mistakes, most Python package index systems, including PyPI, do not let these wheels be uploaded.

Uploadable Python wheels must be tagged with a proper platform tag, which shows which versions of the GNU C Library they are compatible with. Historically, those tags relied on the CentOS release year: manylinux1 corresponded to CentOS 5, `manylinux20210` corresponded to CentOS 6, and manylinux20214 corresponded to CentOS 7.

At the time of writing, manylinux_2_24 and manylinux_2_27 are the only post–CentOS 7 versions. These correspond to Debian 9 and Ubuntu 18.04, respectively.

After deciding on the oldest supported platform tag, build on the newest system which supports it. For example, if no deployment target uses GNU C Library < `2.24`, build the wheel until Debian 9. Especially for binary wheels with complicated build dependencies, a newer system makes it easier to follow the documentation and reduces the chances of running into unexpected issues.

2.5.3 manylinux Containers

Making sure that the `patchelf` tool is correctly installed and Python is built with the correct version of the C library is a subtle and error-prone process. One way to avoid this is to use the official manylinux container images.

These container images are available at `quay/pypa/manylinux_<version>`. There are versions available for manylinux_2_24, manylinux2014, manylinux2010, and manylinux1. These images contain all officially supported versions of Python and the rest of the tooling necessary.

Note that specialized build dependencies need to be installed on those systems; for example, when using manylinux_2_24 (a Debian-based container).

```
$ docker run --rm -it quay/pypa/manylinux_2_24
# apt-get update
# apt-get install -y <dependencies>
```

2.5.4 Installing manylinux Wheels

By default, `pip` uses manylinux wheels with compatible platform tags. Wheels can be uploaded to a package index or added to a directory passed to `pip` with `--find-links`.

In some situations, it is better if `pip` fails quickly when no prebuilt wheel is available. The `--only-binary :all:` option can be given to disable installing from source distributions.

2.6 tox

tox is a tool to automatically manage virtual environments, usually for tests and builds. It is used to make sure that those run in well-defined environments and is smart about caching them to reduce churn. True to its roots as a test-running tool, tox is configured in *test environments*.

tox *itself* is a PyPI package usually installed in a virtual environment. Because tox creates ad hoc temporary virtual environments for testing, the virtual environment tox is installed in can be common to many projects. A common pattern is to create a virtual environment dedicated to tox.

```
$ python -m venv ~/.venvs/tox
$ ~/.venvx/tox/bin/python -m pip install tox
$ alias tox=~/.venvs/tox/bin/tox
```

It uses a unique ini-based configuration format. This can make writing configurations difficult since remembering the subtleties of the file format can be hard. However, while hard to tap, there is a lot of power that can certainly configure tests and build clear and concise runs.

One thing that tox lacks is a notion of *dependencies* between build steps. This means that those are usually managed from the outside by running specific test runs after others and sharing artifacts somewhat ad hoc.

A tox *environment* more or less corresponds to a section in the configuration file. By default, tox uses the tox.ini file.

```
[testenv:some-name]
```

-
-
-

Note that if the name of the environment contains pyNM (for example, py36), then tox defaults to using CPython, the standard Python implementation, version N.M (3.6, in this case) as the Python interpreter for that test environment.

tox also supports name-based environment guessing for more esoteric implementations of Python. For example, PyPy, an implementation of Python in Python, is supported with the name pypyNM.

If the name does not include one of the supported short names, or if there is a need to override the default, a basepython field in the section can be used to indicate a specific Python version. By default, tox looks for Python available in the path. However, if the plug-in tox-pyenv is installed in the virtual environment that tox itself is installed in, tox will query pyenv if it cannot find the right Python on the path.

Let's analyze a few tox configuration files in order of increasing complexity.

2.6.1 One Environment

In this example, there is only one test environment. This test environment uses Python 3.9.

```
[tox]
envlist = py39
```

The tox section is a global configuration. In this example, the only global configuration is the list of environments.

```
[testenv]
```

This section configures the test environment. Since there is only one test environment, there is no need for a separate configuration.

```
deps =
    flake8
```

The deps subsection details which packages should be installed in the virtual test environment. Here the configuration specifies flake8 with a loose dependency. Another option is to specify a strict dependency; for example, flake8==1.0.0..

This helps with reproducible test runs. It could also specify -r <requirements file> and manage them separately. This is useful when there is another tool that takes the requirements file.

```
commands =
    flake8 useful
```

In this case, the only command is to run flake8 in the useful directory. By default, a tox test run succeeds if all commands return a successful status code. As something designed to run from command lines, flake8 respects this convention and only exits with a successful status code if there are no problems detected with the code.

2.6.2 Multiple Environments

In the following examples, the tox configuration runs unit tests against both Python 3.9 and Python 3.8. This is common for libraries that need to support more than one version.

```
[tox]
envlist = py39,py38
```

The two environments can share configuration. Even though there is no configuration difference, they are not redundant. They run the tests against different versions of the interpreter.

```
[testenv]
deps =
    pytest
    hypothesis
    pyhamcrest
commands =
    pytest useful
```

In this environment, tox is configured to install the pytest runner and two testing helper libraries. The tox.ini file documents the assumptions on the tools needed to run the tests.

The command to be run is short. The pytest tool also respects the testing tools convention and only exit successfully if there are no test failures.

2.6.3 Multiple Differently Configured Environments

As a more realistic example, let's turn to the tox.ini of ncolony.

```
[tox]
envlist = {py38,py39}-{unit,func},py39-wheel,docs
toxworkdir = {toxinidir}/build/.tox
```

It is possible to define environments in a matrix way like this. The environments to be created are py38-unit, py38-func, py39-unit, and py39-func.

This becomes more useful the more environments there are. This is also a way to make *too many* environments. For example, {py37,py38,py39}-{unit,func}-{olddeps,newdeps}-{mindeps,maxdeps} creates 3*2*2*2*2=24 environments, which takes a toll when running the tests.

The numbers for a matrix test like this climb up fast; using an automated test environment means things would either take longer or need higher parallelism.

This is a normal trade-off between the comprehensiveness of testing and resource use. There is no magic solution other than carefully considering how many variations to officially support.

Instead of having a separate testenv-<name> configuration section per environment, it is possible to use one section and special-case the environments using matching. This is a more efficient way to create many similar versions of test environments.

```
[testenv]
deps =
    {py38,py39}-unit: coverage
    {py38,py39}-{func,unit}: twisted
    {py38,py39}-{func,unit}: ncolony
```

The coverage tool is only used for unit tests. The Twisted and ncolony libraries are needed for unit and functional tests.

```
commands =
    {py38,py39}-unit: python -Wall \
                                 -Wignore::DeprecationWarning \
                                 -m coverage \
                                 run -m twisted.trial \
                                 --temp-directory build/_trial_temp \
                                 {posargs:ncolony}
    {py38,py39}-unit: coverage report --include ncolony* \
                        --omit */tests/*,*/interfaces*,*/_version* \
                                --show-missing --fail-under=100
    {py38,py39}-func: python -Werror -W ignore::DeprecationWarning \
                                -W ignore::ImportWarning \
                                -m ncolony tests.functional_test
```

Configuring one big test environment means all the commands are in one bag and selected based on patterns. This is also a more realistic test run command, including warnings configuration, coverage, and arguments to the test runner.

While the exact complications vary, there are almost always enough things that lead the commands to grow to a decent size.

The following environment is different enough that it makes sense to break it out into its own section.

```
[testenv:py39-wheel]
skip_install = True
deps =
    build
commands =
    python -c 'import os, sys;os.makedirs(sys.argv[1])" {envtmpdir}/dist
    python -m build --outdir {envtmpdir}/dist --no-isolation
```

The py39-wheel section ensures that the wheel can be built. A more sophisticated configuration might install the wheel and run the unit tests.

Finally, the docs section builds the documentation. This helps avoid syntax errors resulting in the documentation failing to build.

```
[testenv:docs]
changedir = docs
deps =
    sphinx
commands =
    sphinx-build -W -b html -d {envtmpdir}/doctrees . {envtmpdir}/html
basepython = python3.9
```

For it to run, it needs to have a docs subdirectory with a conf.py and, depending on the contexts of the configuration file, more files. Note that basepython must be explicitly declared in this case since it is not part of the environment's name.

The documentation build is one of the reasons why tox shines. It only installs sphinx in the virtual environment for building documentation. This means that an undeclared dependency on sphinx would make the unit tests fail since sphinx is not installed there.

2.7 Pip Tools

The pip-tools PyPI package contains a dedicated command to freeze dependencies. The pip-compile command takes a loose requirements file as an input and produces one with strict requirements.

The usual names for the files are requirements.in for the input and requirements. txt for the output. Sometimes, when there are a few related variations of dependencies, the files are called requirements-<purpose>.in and requirements-<purpose>.txt, respectively.

There are two common purposes.

- dev: packages needed for development, but not while running

- test: packages needed for testing but not running regularly

Running the command can be as simple as the following.

```
$ pip-compile < requirements.in > requirements.txt
...
```

More commonly, the loose requirements are already in a setup.cfg for the local code that uses the libraries. In those cases, pip-compile can take this as input directly.

For example, a setup.cfg file for a web application might have a dependency on gunicorn and a *test* dependency on pytest.

```
[options]
install_requires=
    gunicorn
[options.extras_require]
test =
    pytest
```

The pip-compile commands also need a trivial setup.py.

```
import setuptools
setuptools.setup()
```

It is usually best to also have a pyproject.toml, though it can be empty. Even though pip-compile does not depend on it, it does help with other parts of the workflow.

In such a case, pip-compile uses the package metadata automatically.

```
$ pip-compile > requirements.txt
<output snipped>
$ sed -e 's/ *#.*//' -e '/^$/d' requirements.txt
gunicorn==20.1.0
```

The output, `requirements.txt`, contains quite a few comment lines. The only non-comment line is the pinned `gunicorn` dependency. Note that the version is different when running `pip-compile` again in the future when a new package has been released.

It is also possible to generate the `requirements-test.txt` file by running `pip-compile` with the `--extra` argument.

```
$ pip-compile --extra test > requirements-test.txt
<output snipped>
$ sed -e 's/ *#.*//' -e '/^$/d' requirements.txt
attrs==21.4.0
gunicorn==20.1.0
iniconfig==1.1.1
packaging==21.3
pluggy==1.0.0
py==1.11.0
pyparsing==3.0.6
pytest==6.2.5
toml==0.10.2
```

This time, the `pytest` dependency generated more dependencies. All dependencies are pinned.

Note that while `pip-tools` does try to replicate the algorithm `pip` uses, there are some edge cases in which the resolution differs, or one might fail to find a resolution. This tends to happen in edge cases, and one way to improve things is to add specificity to some of the dependencies, often as `>=` details.

Note that even this relatively simple (hypothetical) Python program with two direct dependencies had nine total dependencies. This is typical; frozen, complete dependencies often number in the tens for simple programs and hundreds for many code bases.

Although `requirements.txt` and `requirements-*.txt` are *generated* files, checking them into the source code for applications is usually recommended. For libraries, it sometimes makes sense to check in `requirements-test.txt` to run at least one set of tests with known-good dependencies.

In either case, it is good to refresh the dependencies occasionally. Most libraries only fix bugs, and security issues, at their tip. Being too far behind the latest version means that if a bug fix or security patch becomes important, a library upgrade is potentially needed. These upgrades tend to be harder. Even with perfectly executed semantic versioning, the library might have bumped its major version number. More realistically, even without a major version number, some assumptions might be wrong. The bigger the jump, the more these assumptions interact and become complicated to resolve.

There are services that automatically open pull requests updating `requirements.txt`. If none of those are feasible to use, for any reason, writing a script that re-runs `pip-compile` and produces a pull request is possible. In that case, use the `-U` flag to `pip-compile` to let it know that all dependencies need to be upgraded to the latest mutually-consistent versions.

The most important thing is to do it regularly and merge the resulting pull request. These pull requests need to be treated as carefully, if not more so, than those that change the Python code itself. Whatever workflow is used for the latter is appropriate for these dependency-bump pull requests.

2.8 Poetry

Poetry is a package and dependency management system. It gives one tool which handles the entire Python development process: managing dependencies, creating virtual environments, building and publishing packages, and installing Python applications.

2.8.1 Installing

There are several ways to install Poetry. One is by using a `get-poetry.py` script, which uses Python to install Poetry locally.

This can be done by piping it straight into Python.

```
$ curl -sSL \
```

```
https://raw.githubusercontent.com/python-poetry/poetry/master/get-
poetry.py \
| python -
```

It is also possible to download the script with `curl -o get-poetry.py ...` and then run it.

In some circumstances, it might make sense to install Poetry into a dedicated virtual environment, using `pip install poetry` in the virtual environment. One advantage of the `pip`-based installation method is that it works with a local Python package index. This is sometimes useful for compliance or security reasons.

Regardless of how it was installed, `poetry self update` updates Poetry to the latest version. It is also possible to update to a specific version as a parameter to the `update` command.

For shell completions, `poetry completions <shell name>` outputs shellcode for completions compatible with the given shell. This can be loaded globally or per user as appropriate for the relevant shell. Among the shells supported are `bash`, `zsh`, and `fish`.

2.8.2 Creating

Usually, the best way to start with Poetry is on a fresh project. It can create a skeleton for a Poetry-based project.

```
$ poetry new simple_app
```

This creates a directory called `simple_app` with a minimal Poetry skeleton.

In most cases, this new directory, `simple_app`, is version-controlled. This is not done by `poetry new`, so it is a good idea to do it immediately after; for example, using `git`.

```
$ git init .
$ git add .        .
$ git commit -a -m 'Output of "poetry new"'
```

The most important file is `pyproject.toml` at the root of the directory. It contains the `build-system` section.

```
[build-system]
requires = ["poetry-core>=1.0.0"]
build-backend = "poetry.core.masonry.api"
```

This makes it compatible with python -m build for building wheels and source distributions.

The pyproject.toml file also contains some Poetry-specific sections, all marked by having tool.poetry as a prefix. The main section, tool.poetry, contains package metadata.

```
[tool.poetry]
name = <name>
version = <version>
description = <description>
authors = ["<author name and e-mail>", ...]
```

The version field can be edited manually, but it is better to use poetry version <bump rule> or poetry version <version> to modify the versions.

```
$ poetry version patch
...
$ git diff
....
--- pyproject.toml
+++ pyproject.toml
@@ -1,6 +1,6 @@
 [tool.poetry]
 name = "simple_app"
-version = "0.1.0"
+version = "0.1.1"
 description = ""
$ poetry version 1.2.3
...
$ git diff
....
--- pyproject.toml
+++ pyproject.toml
@@ -1,6 +1,6 @@
 [tool.poetry]
 name = "simple_app"
-version = "0.1.0"
```

```
+version = "1.2.3"
 description = ""
```

The following are other files that are created.

- README.rst is a bare-bones README.

- <name>/__init__.py is a top-level file that makes the <name>
  directory a package. It also defines an __version__ variable.

- Testing files

  - tests/test_<name>.py is a minimal test checking that the version number
    is valid. Its main utility is that poetry run pytest does not fail.

  - tests/__init__.py is a file that does not contain tests. Making the tests
    directory into a package is required for the way Poetry runs pytest.

2.8.3 Dependencies

Assume that the goal of simple_app is to be a Pyramid-based web application that runs
with gunicorn. The first step is to add those dependencies to Poetry. The pyramid add
subcommand adds dependencies.

```
$ poetry add pyramid gunicorn
```

This modifies the tool.poetry.dependencies section in pyproject.toml as follows.

```
[tool.poetry.dependencies]
python = "^3.8"
pyramid = "^2.0"
gunicorn = "^20.1.0"
```

By default, Poetry assumes that the dependencies are semantically versioned. This
means that potential security fixes can be fixed if they are not backported to previous
versions. Most Python packages do not backport fixes, so this is something to be
careful with.

This command also creates the poetry.lock file, which has recursively-complete
pinned dependencies. These are the dependencies used by Poetry. The poetry lock
command updates the pinned dependencies.

It is possible to export those locked dependencies to a requirements.txt file.

```
$ poetry export > requirements.txt
```

Depending on what the package is used for, either poetry.lock, requirements.txt, or both should be checked into source control.

2.8.4 Developing

Even a minimally functional Pyramid app requires a little more code.

```python
# simple_app/web.py
from pyramid import config, response
def root(request):
    return response.Response("Useful string")
with config.Configurator() as cfg:
    cfg.add_route("root", "/")
    cfg.add_view(root, route_name='root')
    application = cfg.make_wsgi_app()
```

Since the pyramid and gunicorn dependencies are already in Poetry, it can directly run the code. There is no need to explicitly create a virtual environment.

```
$ poetry run gunicorn simple_app.web
[2021-09-25 14:26:29 -0700] [2190296] [INFO] Starting gunicorn 20.1.0
...
```

Similarly, to run tests, use poetry run pytest.

2.8.5 Building

The poetry build command generates a source distribution and a wheel under dist. Alternatively, python -m build does the same.

```
$ pip install build
...
$ python -m build
...
Successfully built simple_app-0.1.0.tar.gz and simple_app-0.1.0-py3-none-any.whl
```

The latter is useful when building wheels inside a minimal OS, say a container. In that case, installing Poetry in addition to Python might be too awkward or complicated.

Whether by `poetry build` or `python -m build`, the wheel package can be installed without requiring Poetry. This is true whether the wheel is uploaded to a package index and installed from there or installed using `pip install <path to wheel>`.

Note that the wheel has the loose dependencies defined in `pyproject.toml`. To install pinned dependencies, use Poetry to install or prefix the wheel installation with `pip install -r requirements.txt`. This requires exporting the `poetry.lock` dependencies to `requirements.txt`, as shown earlier.

2.9 Pipenv

Pipenv is a tool to create virtual environments that match a specification and ways to evolve the specification. It relies on two files: `Pipfile` and `Pipfile.lock`.

A popular way to install Pipenv is in a custom virtual environment. Usually, it is best to run it from this virtual environment *inactivated*. This can be done using a command-line-level alias.

```
$ python3 -m venv ~/.venvs/pipenv
$ ~/.venvs/pipenv/bin/pip install pipenv
$ alias pipenv=~/.venvs/pipenv/bin/pipenv
```

If you intend to run Pipenv from an activated virtual environment, the `PIPENV_IGNORE_VIRTUALENVS` environment variable should be set to 1.

```
$ export PIPENV_IGNORE_VIRTUALENVS=1
$ . ~/.venvs/pipenv/bin/activate
```

Pipenv assumes that it controls a project's directory. To start using it, create a new directory. Inside this directory, it is possible to install packages using `pipenv add`.

To run code that uses the packages, use `pipenv shell`. This is similar to activating a virtual environment, but it opens a *new shell*. Instead of deactivating the environment, exit the shell.

```
$ mkdir useful
$ cd useful
$ pipenv add termcolor
```

```
$ mkdir useful
$ touch useful/__init__.py
$ cat > useful/__main__.py
import termcolor
print(termcolor.colored("Hello", "red"))
$ pipenv shell
(pipenv)$ python -m useful
(pipenv)$ exit
$
```

This leaves in its wake a `Pipfile` that looks like the following.

```
[[source]]
url = "https://pypi.org/simple"
verify_ssl = true
name = "pypi"

[packages]
termcolor = "*"

[dev-packages]

[requires]
python_version = "3.8"
```

The Pipenv tool is not used for building packages. It is strictly a tool to improve local development or create virtual environments for deployment. For `useful` to be shippable distribution, in this case, it would need a `setup.cfg` and `pyproject.toml`.

2.10 DevPI

DevPI is a PyPI-compatible server that can be run locally. Though it does not scale to PyPI-like levels, it can be a powerful tool in several situations.

DevPI is made up of three parts. The most important one is `devpi-server`. For many use cases, this is the only part that needs to run. The server serves, first and foremost, as a caching proxy to PyPI. It takes advantage of the fact that packages on PyPI are *immutable*: once you have a package, it can never change.

There is also a web server that allows you to search in the local package directory. Since many use cases do not even involve searching on the PyPI website, this is optional. Finally, there is a client command-line tool that allows configuring various parameters on the running instance. The client is most useful in more esoteric use cases.

Installing and running DevPI is straightforward. In a virtual environment, simply run

```
(devpi)$ pip install devpi-server
(devpi)$ devpi-init
(devpi)$ devpi-server
```

The `pip` tool, by default, goes to `pypi.org`. For some basic testing of DevPI, you can create a new virtual environment, `playground`, and run

```
(playground)$ pip install \
              -i http://localhost:3141/root/pypi/+simple/ \
              httpie glom
(playground)$ http --body https://httpbin.org/get | glom '{"url":"url"}'
{
  "url": "https://httpbin.org/get"
}
```

Having to specify the `-i ...` argument to `pip` every time would be annoying. After checking that everything worked correctly, you can put the configuration in an environment variable.

```
$ export PIP_INDEX_URL=http://localhost:3141/root/pypi/+simple/
```

To make things more permanent, configure a `pip.conf` file.

```
[global]
index-url = http://localhost:3141/root/pypi/+simple/

[search]
index = http://localhost:3141/root/pypi/
```

It is possible to put `pip.conf` in the root of a virtual environment to test it. To make it permanent, for example, if working on a computer that often loses connectivity, uses the user-specific `pip.conf`.

- Unix: `~/.pip/pip.conf`

- macOS: `$HOME/Library/Application Support/pip/pip.conf`.

- Windows: `%APPDATA%\pip\pip.ini`.

To apply it to all users, edit `/etc/pip.conf` on Unix. This can be useful, for example, when building container images against a DevPI.

DevPI is useful for disconnected operations. To install packages without a network, DevPI can be used to cache them. As mentioned earlier, virtual environments are disposable and often treated as mostly immutable. This means that a virtual environment with the right packages *is not* useful without a network. The chances are high that some situations will either require or suggest creating it from scratch.

However, a caching server is a different matter. If all package retrieval is done through a caching proxy, then destroying a virtual environment and rebuilding it is fine since the source of truth is the package cache. This is as useful for taking a laptop into the woods for disconnected development as maintaining proper firewall boundaries and having a consistent record of all installed software.

To warm up the DevPI cache (i.e., make sure it contains all needed packages), you need to use `pip` to install them. One way to do it is, after configuring DevPI and `pip`, to run tox against a source repository of software under development. Since tox goes through all test environments, it downloads all needed packages.

It is a good practice to also preinstall any `requirements.txt` files that are relevant in a disposable virtual environment.

However, the utility of DevPI is not limited to disconnected operations. Configuring one inside your build cluster, and pointing the build cluster at it, completely avoids the risk of a left-pad incident, where a package you rely on gets removed by the author from PyPI. It might also make builds faster and cut out a lot of outgoing traffic.

Another use for DevPI is to test uploads before uploading them to PyPI. Assuming `devpi-server` is already running on the default port, it is possible to upload a package using `twine`. Usually, this is a package that is being tested, but as a test, it reuploads the popular `boltons` package.

```
(devpi)$ pip install devpi-client twine
(devpi)$ devpi use http://localhost:3141
(devpi)$ devpi user -c testuser password=123
(devpi)$ devpi login testuser --password=123
(devpi)$ devpi index -c dev bases=root/pypi
```

```
(devpi)$ devpi use testuser/dev
(devpi)$ pip download boltons==21.0.0
(devpi)$ twine upload --repository-url http://localhost:3141/testuser/dev \
              -u testuser -p 123 boltons-21.0.0-py2.py3-none-any.whl
(devpi)$ pip install -i http://localhost:3141/testuser/dev my-package
```

Note that this allows you to upload to an index that you only use explicitly, so you are not shadowing my-package for all environments that are not using this explicitly.

In an even more advanced use case, you can do the following.

```
(devpi)$ devpi index root/pypi mirror_url=https://ourdevpi.local
```

This makes your DevPI server a mirror of a local, upstream DevPI server. This allows you to upload private packages to the central DevPI server to share with your team. In those cases, the upstream DevPI server often needs to be run behind a proxy, and you need to have some tools to properly manage user access.

Running a centralized DevPI behind a simple proxy that asks for a username and password allows an effective private repository.

For that, create the server without a root index: .. code.

```
$ devpi-init --no-root-pypi
$ devpi login root
...
$ devpi index --create pypi
```

This means the root index no longer mirrors pypi. You can upload packages now directly to it. This type of server is often used with the --extra-index-url argument to pip, allowing pip to retrieve from the private and external sources. However, sometimes it is useful to have a DevPI instance that only serves specific packages. This allows enforcing rules about auditing before using any packages. It is downloaded, audited, and then added to the private repository whenever a new package is needed.

2.11 pex and shiv

While it is non-trivial to compile a Python program into one self-contained executable, you can do something *almost* as good. You can compile a Python program into a single file that only needs an installed interpreter to run. This takes advantage of the particular way Python handles start-ups.

When running python /path/to/filename, Python does two things.

- Adds the /path/to directory to the module path.

- Executes the code in /path/to/filename.

When running python /path/to/directory/, Python acts as though you typed python /path/to/ directory/__main__.py.
In other words, Python does the following two things.

- Add the /path/to/directory/ directory to the module path.

- Executes the code in /path/to/directory/__main__.py.

When running python /path/to/filename.zip, Python treats the file as a directory. In other words, Python does the following two things.

- Add the /path/to/filename.zip directory to the module path.

- Executes the code in the __main__.py it extracts from /path/to/filename.zip.

A zip file is an end-oriented format. The metadata, and pointers to the data, are all at the end. Adding a prefix to a zip file does not change its contents.

So if you take a zip file and prefix it with #!/usr/bin/python<newline>, and mark it executable, then when running it, Python is running a zip file. If you put the right bootstrapping code in __main__.py and the right modules in the zip file, you can get all the third-party dependencies in one big file.

pex and shiv are tools for producing such files, but they both rely on the same underlying behavior of Python and zip files.

2.11.1 pex

pex can be used either as a command-line tool or as a library. When using it as a command-line tool, it is good to prevent it from trying to make dependency resolution against PyPI. All dependency resolution algorithms are flawed in some way. However, packages work around flaws explicitly in their algorithm due to pip's popularity. pex is less popular, and there are no guarantee packages try explicitly to work with it.

The safest thing to do is to use pip wheel to build all wheels in a directory, and then tell pex to use only this directory.

For example,

```
$ pip instal pex
$ pip wheel --wheel-dir my-wheels -r requirements.txt
$ pex -o my-file.pex --find-links my-wheels --no-index \
      -m some_package
```

pex has a few ways to find the entrypoint. The two most popular ones are -m some_package, which behaves like python -m some_package, and -c console-script, which finds which script would have been installed as console-script and invokes the relevant entrypoint.

It is also possible to use pex as a library. This allows writing Python code, rather than using shell automation, to build a pex file.

```
from pex import pex_builder
import sys, subprocess

builder = pex_builder.PEXBuilder()
builder.set_entry_point('some_package')
builder.set_shebang(sys.executable)
subprocess.check_call([sys.executable, '-m', 'pip', 'wheel',
                       '--wheel-dir', 'my-wheels',
                       '-requirements', 'requirements.txt'])
for dist in os.listdir('my-wheels'):
    dist = os.path.join('my-wheels', dist)
    builder.add_dist_location(dist)
builder.build('my-file.pex')
```

This code is largely equivalent to the earlier shell lines. The .set_entry_point() method is the equivalent of the -m argument.

This example sets the shebang line explicitly to sys.executable. By default, pex uses a sophisticated algorithm to get a good shebang line. This example overrode it, choosing to be explicit about using the interpreter.

The shebang line is sometimes specific to the expected deployment environment, so it is good to put some thought into it. One option is /usr/bin/env python, which finds what the current shell calls python.

Note that even though this is Python code, it creates wheels by starting `pip` as a process. The `pip` tool is not usable as a library; calling it a process is the only supported interface.

While this is more code than a few shell commands, having it in Python means that as the build process becomes more sophisticated, it is unnecessary to write complicated code in shell.

2.11.2 shiv

shiv is a modern take on the same ideas behind pex. However, since it uses `pip` directly, it needs to do a lot less itself.

```
$ pip install shiv
$ shiv -o my-file.shiv -e some_package -r requirements.txt
```

Because shiv just off-loads to pip actual dependency resolution, it is safe to call it directly. shiv is a younger alternative to pex. A lot of cruft has been removed, but it is still lacking somewhat in maturity.

For example, the documentation for command-line arguments is a bit thin. There is also no way to use it as a library currently.

Note that `shiv` only supports Python 3.6 and above.

2.12 Summary

Much of the power of Python comes from its powerful third-party ecosystems. Whether for data science or networking code, there are many good options. Understanding how to install, use, and update third-party packages is crucial to using Python well.

With private package repositories, using Python packages for internal libraries, and distributing them in a way compatible with open source libraries, is often a good idea. It allows using the same machinery for internal distribution, versioning, and dependency management.

CHAPTER 3

Interactive Usage

Python is often used for exploratory programming. Often, the result is not the program but an answer to a question. For scientists, the question might be about the likelihood of a medical intervention working. For people troubleshooting computers, the question might be which log file has the message I need.

However, regardless of the question, Python can often be a powerful tool to answer it. More importantly, in exploratory programming, you can expect to encounter more questions based on the answer.

The interactive model in Python comes from the original Lisp environment, Read-Eval-Print Loop (REPL). The environment reads a Python expression, evaluates it in an environment that persists in memory, prints the result, and loops back.

The REPL environment native to Python is popular because it is built-in. However, a few third-party REPL tools are even more powerful, built to do things that the native one could not or would not. These tools give a powerful way to interact with the operating system, exploring and molding until the desired state is achieved.

The basic console has the advantage of being built-in; it is available wherever Python is. As well as being available for direct usage, it can also be directly customized from Python using the code built-in module, allowing organization-specific Python REPL.

The IPython and ptpython interactive environments focus on enhancing the interactive console experience. IPython focuses on extensibility and history, while ptpython focuses on using the terminal's capabilities to deliver a top-notch UI experience.

Jupyter uses the universal browser UI to have a REPL that supports inline graphical output, interactive UI elements like buttons and text inputs, and support for an IPython-like in-browser experience that shares the same Python environment. Jupyter also supports notebooks, a way to save a REPL session in a shareable way. These notebooks can be attached to tickets or even checked into source control. Most modern source control environments directly render the notebooks, making them ideal as teaching and collaboration tools.

© Moshe Zadka 2022
M. Zadka, *DevOps in Python*, https://doi.org/10.1007/978-1-4842-7996-0_3

3.1 Native Console

Launching Python without any arguments opens the interactive console. It is a good idea to use pyenv or a virtual environment to make sure that the correct Python version is up to date. Some operating systems have a default version of Python running a legacy version of Python.

The availability of an interactive console immediately, without installing anything else, is one reason why Python is suited for exploratory programming. The interpreter can immediately answer questions.

The questions can be trivial.

```
>>> 2 + 2
4
```

They can be used to calculate sales tax in the San Francisco Bay Area.

```
>>> rate = 9.25
>>> price = 5.99
>>> after_tax = price * (1 + rate / 100.)
>>> after_tax
6.544075
```

They can answer important questions about the operating environment.

```
>>> import os
>>> os.path.isfile(os.path.expanduser("~/.bashrc"))
True
```

This checks whether the user has `.bashrc` in their home directory; it is true for some users on some systems and false for others.

Pythons native console using the GNU readline library to afford editing. If `python -c 'import readline'` fails with an `ImportError`, Python was not built with readline support, leading to a degraded experience at the console. If rebuilding Python with readline support is not an option (for example, using a locally built Python by a different team), it is highly recommended to use one of the alternative consoles described in this chapter.

If readline support is installed, Python uses it to support line editing and history. It is also possible to save the history using `readline.write_history_file`.

```
>>> import readline, os
>>> readline.write_history_file(os.path.expanduser("~/.python-history"))
```

This can be useful after having used the console for a while. The history file can serve as a reference for what has been done or copy whatever ideas worked into a more permanent form.

When using the console, the _ variable has the value of the last expression statement evaluated. Note that exceptions, statements that are not expressions, and statements that are expressions that evaluate to None do not change the value of _. This is useful during an interactive session when only after having seen the representation of the value that you realize you needed it as an object.

```
>>> import requests
>>> requests.get("http://en.wikipedia.org")
<Response [200]>
>>> a=_
>>> a.text[:50]
'<!DOCTYPE html>\n<html class="client-nojs" lang="en'
```

After using the .get function, you realize that what you wanted was the text. Luckily, the Response object is saved in the _ variable. The value of the variable is put in a immediately because: _ is replaced quickly. As soon as you evaluate a.text[:50], _ is a 50-character string. If you had not saved _ in a variable, all but the first 50 characters would have been lost.

Notice that every good Python REPL keeps this _ convention, and so the trick of keeping returned values in one-letter variables is often useful when doing explorations.

3.2 The Code Module

The code module allows you to run your own interactive loop. An example of when this can be useful is when running commands with a special flag. You can drop into a prompt at a specific point, allowing you to have a REPL environment after setting things up in a certain way. This holds for both inside the interpreter, setting up the namespace with useful things, and in the external environment, perhaps initializing files or setting up external services.

The highest-level use of code is the interact function.

```
>>> import code
>>> code.interact(banner="Welcome to the special interpreter",
...              local=dict(special=[1, 2, 3]))
Welcome to the special interpreter
>>> special
[1, 2, 3]
>>> ^D
now exiting InteractiveConsole...
>>> special
Traceback (most recent call last):
  File "<stdin>", line 1, in <module>
NameError: name 'special' is not defined
```

This example is running a REPL loop with a special variable, which is set to a short list. To get out of the inner-interpreter, press Control+D (indicated as ^D).

For the lowest-level use of code, allowing complete ownership of the UI, code. compile_command(source, [filename="<input>"], symbol="single") returns a code object (that can be passed to exec), None if the command is incomplete, or raises SyntaxError, OverflowError, or ValueError if there is a problem with the command.

The symbol argument should almost always be "single". The exception is if the user is prompted to enter code that evaluates an expression (for example, if the value is to be used by the underlying system). In that case, symbol should be set to "eval".

This allows you to manage interaction with users. It can be integrated with a UI, or a remote network interface, to allow interactivity in any environment.

3.3 ptpython

The ptpython tool, short for prompt toolkit Python, is an alternative to the built-in REPL. It uses the prompt toolkit for console interaction, instead of readline.

Its main advantage is the simplicity of installation. A simple pip install ptpython in a virtual environment, and regardless of readline build problems, a high-quality Python REPL appears.

ptpython supports completion suggestions, multiline editing, and syntax highlighting.

On start-up, it reads `~/.ptpython/config.py`, which means it is possible to locally customize ptpython in arbitrary ways. To configure, implement a `configure` function, which accepts an object (of type `PythonRepl`) and mutates it.

There are a lot of possibilities, and sadly the only real documentation is the source code. The relevant reference `__init__` is `ptpython.python_input.PythonInput`. Note that `config.py` is an arbitrary Python file. Therefore, if you want to distribute modifications internally, it is possible to distribute a local PyPI package and have people import a `configure` function from it.

3.4 IPython

IPython, the foundation of Jupyter, is an interactive environment whose roots are in the scientific computing community. IPython is an interactive command prompt, similar to the ptpython utility or Python's native REPL.

However, it aims to give a sophisticated environment. One of the things it does is number every input and output from the interpreter. It is useful to be able to refer to those numbers later. IPython puts all inputs in the In array and outputs in the Out array. This allows for nice symmetry if IPython says In[4], for example. The following shows how to access that value.

```
$ ipython
Python 3.10.1 (main, Dec 21 2021, 09:01:08) [GCC 10.2.1 20210110]
Type 'copyright', 'credits' or 'license' for more information
IPython 7.30.1 -- An enhanced Interactive Python. Type '?' for help.

In [1]: print("hello")
hello

In [2]: In[1]
Out[2]: 'print("hello")'

In [3]: 5 + 4.0
Out[3]: 9.0

In [4]: Out[3] == 9.0
Out[4]: True
```

It also supports tab completion out of the box. IPython uses both its own completion and the `jedi` library for static completion.

It also supports built-in help. Entering `var_name?` attempts to find the best context-relevant help for the object in the variable and display it. This works for functions, classes, built-in objects, and more.

```
In [1]: list?
Init signature: list(self, /, *args, **kwargs)
Docstring:
list() -> new empty list
list(iterable) -> new list initialized from iterable's items
Type:           type
```

IPython also supports Magics commands, where prefixing a line with `%` executes a magic function; for example, `%run` runs a Python script inside the current namespace. As another example, `%edit` launches an editor. This is useful if a statement needs more sophisticated editing.

In addition, prefixing a line with `!` runs a system command. One useful way to take advantage of this is `!pip install something`. This is why installing IPython inside virtual environments used for interactive development is useful.

IPython can be customized in a number of ways. While in an interactive session, the `%config` magic command can be used to change any option. For example, `%config InteractiveShell.autocall = True` sets the autocall option, which means callable expressions are called, even without parentheses. This is moot for any options that only affect startup. You can change these options, as well as any others, using the command line. For example, `ipython --InteractiveShell.autocall=True`, launches into an autocalling interpreter.

If you want custom logic to decide on configuration, you can run IPython from a specialized Python script.

```
from traitlets import config
import IPython

my_config = config.Config()
my_config.InteractiveShell.autocall = True

IPython.start_ipython(config=my_config)
```

If this is in a dedicated Python package, you can distribute it to a team using PyPI or a private package repository. This allows a homogenous custom IPython configuration for a development team.

Finally, a configuration can also be encoded in profiles, which are Python snippets located under `~/.ipython` by default. The profile directory can be modified by an explicit `--ipython-dir` command-line parameter or an `IPYTHONDIR` environment variable.

3.5 JupyterLab

Jupyter is a project that uses web-based interaction to allow for sophisticated exploratory programming. It is not limited to Python, though it does originate in Python. The name is short for Julia/Python/R, the three languages most popular for exploratory programming, especially data science.

JupyterLab, the latest evolution of Jupyter, was originally based on IPython. It now sports a full-featured web interface and a way to edit files remotely. The main users of Jupyter tend to be scientists. They take advantage of seeing how results were derived to add reproducibility and peer review.

Reproducibility and peer-review are also important for DevOps work. The ability to show the steps that led to deciding which list of hosts to restart so that it can be regenerated if circumstances change, for example, is highly useful. The ability to attach a notebook detailing the steps taken during an outage, together with the output from the steps, to a post-mortem analysis can aid in understanding what happened and how to avoid a problem in the future or recover from it more effectively.

It is important to note here that notebooks are *not* an auditability tool. They can be executed out of order and have blocks modified and re-executed. However, properly used, they allow you to record what has been done.

Jupyter allows true exploratory programming, which is useful for scientists who might not understand the true scope of a problem beforehand.

This is also useful for systems integrators faced with complex systems where it is hard to predict where the problem lies before exploration.

Installing JupyterLab in a virtual environment is a simple matter of typing `pip install jupyterlab`. By default, it starts a web server on an open port starting at 8888 and attempts to launch a web browser to watch it. If working on an environment that is too interesting (for example, the default web browser is not configured properly), the standard output contains a preauthorized URL to access the server. If all else fails, it is possible to copy-paste the token printed to standard output into the browser after manually entering the URL in a web browser. It is also possible to access the token with `jupyter notebook list`, which lists all currently running servers.

Once inside JupyterLab, there are four things you can launch.

- Console

- Terminal

- Text editor

- Notebook

- Spreadsheet editor

The console is a web-based interface to IPython. All that was said about IPython previously (for example, the `In` and `Out` arrays). The terminal is a full-fledged terminal emulator in the browser. This is useful for a remote terminal inside a VPN. All it needs as far as connectivity needs is an open web port. It can also be protected in the regular ways web ports are protected: TLS, client-side certificates, and more. The text editor is useful for similar reasons; this avoids the need to run `vi` through a shell to a remote location, resulting in lag, while full file editing capabilities still exist.

The most interesting thing to launch is a notebook; indeed, many sessions use nothing but notebooks. A notebook is a JSON file that records a session. As the session unfolds, Jupyter saves snapshots of the notebook and the latest version. A notebook is made of a sequence of cells. The two most popular cell types are Code and Markdown. A code cell type contains a Python code snippet. It executes it in the context of the session's namespace. The namespace is persistent from one cell execution to the other, corresponding to a kernel running. The kernel accepts cell content using a custom protocol, interprets them as Python, executes them, and returns whatever was returned by the snippet and the output.

By default, a Jupyter server uses the local IPython kernel as its only possible kernel. This means that the server can only use the same Python version and the same set of packages. However, connecting a kernel from a different environment to this server is possible. The only requirement is that the environment has the ipykernel package installed. From the environment, run

```
python -m ipykernel install \
      --name my-special-env \
      --display-name "My Env" \
      --prefix=$DIRECTORY
```

Then, from the Jupyter server environment, run

```
jupyter kernelspec install \
      $DIRECTORY/share/jupyter/kernels/my-special-env \
      --sys-prefix
```

This causes the Jupyter server in this environment to support the kernel from the special environment. The --sys-prefix installs it inside the virtual environment where Jupyter is installed.

This allows running one semi-permanent Jupyter server and connecting kernels from any interesting environment. Environments can be interesting because they have specific modules installed or run a specific Python version.

Alternative languages are another usage of alternative kernels. Julia and R kernels are supported upstream, but third-party kernels exist for many languages—even bash!

Jupyter supports all magic commands from IPython. Especially useful, again, is the !pip install ... command to install new packages in the virtual environment. Especially if being careful and installing precise dependencies, this makes a notebook be high-quality documentation of how to achieve a result in a replayable way.

Since Jupyter is one level of indirection away from the kernel, you can restart the kernel directly from Jupyter. This means the whole Python process gets restarted, and any in-memory results are gone. You can re-execute cells in any order, but there is a single-button way to execute all cells in order. Restarting the kernel, and executing all cells in order, is a nice way of testing a notebook for working conditions. Although, naturally, any effects on the external world are not reset.

Jupyter notebooks are useful as attachments to tickets and post-mortems, both as a way of documenting specific remediations and documenting the state of things by running query APIs and collecting the results in the notebook. Usually, when attaching a notebook in such a way, it is useful to export it to a more easily readable format, such as HTML or PDF, and attach that. However, more and more tools integrate direct notebook viewing, making this step redundant. For example, GitHub projects and Gists already render notebooks directly.

JupyterLab sports a rudimentary but functional, browser-based remote development environment. The first part is a remote file manager. Among other things, this allows uploading and downloading files. One use for it, among many, is the ability to upload notebooks from the local computer and download them back again. There are better ways to manage notebooks, but in a pinch, being able to retrieve a notebook is extremely useful. Similarly, any persistent outputs from Jupyter, such as processed data files, images, or charts, can also be downloaded.

Next, alongside the notebooks, is a remote IPython console. Though of limited use next to the notebook, there are still some cases where using the console is easier. A session that requires a lot of short commands can be more keyboard-centric by using the IPython console and thus more efficient.

There is also a file editor. Although it is a far cry from being a full-fledged developer editor, lacking thorough code understanding and completion, it is often useful in a pinch. It allows you to edit files on the remote Jupyter host directly. One use case is directly fixing the library code that the notebook uses and then restarting the kernel. While integrating it into a development flow takes some care, this is invaluable as an emergency measure to fix and continue.

Last, there is a remote browser-based terminal. Between the terminal, the file editor, and the file manager, a running Jupyter server allows complete browser-based remote access and management, even before thinking of the notebooks. This is important for security implications and a powerful tool whose various uses are explored later. For now, suffice it to say, the power that using a Jupyter notebook brings to remote system administration tasks is hard to overestimate.

3.6 Summary

The faster the feedback cycle, the faster you can deploy new, tested solutions. Using Python interactively provides immediate feedback. This is often useful to clarify a library's documentation, a hypothesis about a running system, or your understanding of Python.

The interactive console is also a powerful control panel from which to launch computations when the result is not well understood, for example, when debugging the state of software systems.

CHAPTER 4

OS Automation

Python was initially built to automate a distributed operating system called Amoeba. Although the Amoeba OS is mostly forgotten, Python has found a home in automating Unix-like operating systems tasks.

Python wraps the traditional Unix C API lightly, giving full access to the system calls that run Unix while making them just a little safer to use, an approach that was dubbed "C with foam padding." This willingness to wrap low-level operating system APIs has made it a good choice for the wide berth between the Unix shell programs and the programs the C programming language is good for.

As the saying goes, with great power comes great responsibility. Python does not stop programmers from wreaking havoc to allow programmer power and flexibility. Carefully using Python to write programs that work and, more importantly, break in predictable, safe ways is a skill that is worth mastering.

4.1 Files

It has been a long time since "everything is a file" was an accurate mantra on Unix. Nevertheless, many things are files, and even more things are enough like files that manipulating them with file-based system calls works.

Python programs can go down one of two routes when dealing with a file's contents. They can open a file as text or as binary. Although files are neither text nor binary, just a blob of bytes, the opening mode is important.

When opening a file as binary, the bytes are read and written as byte strings. This is useful with files that are non-textual, such as picture files.

When opening a file as text, *encoding* must be used. It can be specified explicitly, but in certain situations, defaults apply. All bytes read from the file are decoded, and the code receives a *character* string. All strings written to the file are encoded into bytes. This means the interface with the file is with strings, or sequences of characters.

© Moshe Zadka 2022
M. Zadka, *DevOps in Python*, https://doi.org/10.1007/978-1-4842-7996-0_4

A simple example of a binary file is the GIMP XCF internal format. GIMP is an image manipulation program. It saves files in its internal XCF format with more details than images have; for example, layers in the XCF are separate for easy editing.

```
>>> with open("Untitled.xcf", "rb") as fp:
...     header = fp.read(100)
```

Here you open a file. The rb argument stands for "read, binary." You read the first hundred bytes. You need far fewer, but this is often a useful tactic. Many files have some metadata at the beginning.

```
>>> header[:9].decode('ascii')
'gimp xcf '
```

The first nine characters can be decoded to ASCII text and happen to be the name of the format.

```
>>> header[9:9+4].decode('ascii')
'v011'
```

The next four characters are the version. This file is the eleventh version of XCF.

```
>>> header[9+4]
0
```

A 0 byte finishes the "what is this file" metadata. This has various advantages.

```
>>> struct.unpack('>I', header[9+4+1:9+4+1+4])
(1920,)
```

The next four bytes are the width, as a number in big-endian format. The struct module knows how to parse these. The > says it is big-endian, and the I says it is an unsigned 4-byte integer.

```
>>> struct.unpack('>I', header[9+4+1+4:9+4+1+4+4])
(1080,)
```

The next four bytes are the width. This simple code gave you the high-level data, confirming that this is XCF. It showed the format it is, and you could see the dimensions of the image.

When opening files as text, the default encoding is UTF-8. One advantage of UTF-8 is that it is designed to quickly if something is *not* UTF-8. It is carefully designed to fail on ISO-8859-[1–9], which predates Unicode, as well as on most binary files. It is also backward compatible with ASCII, which means pure ASCII files are still valid UTF-8.

The most popular way to parse text files is line by line, and Python supports that by having an open text file be an iterator that yields the lines in order.

```
>>> fp = open("things.txt", "w")
>>> fp.write("""\
... one line
... two lines
... red line
... blue line
... """)
39
>>> fp.close()
>>> fpin = open("things.txt")
>>> next(fpin)
'one linc\n'
>>> next(fpin)
'two lines\n'
>>> next(fpin)
'red line\n'
>>> next(fpin)
'blue line\n'
>>> next(fpin)
Traceback (most recent call last):
  File "<stdin>", line 1, in <module>
StopIteration
```

Usually, you do not call next directly but use for. Additionally, you use files as context managers to make sure they close at a well-understood point. However, there is a trade-off, especially in REPL scenarios; opening the file without a context manager allows you to explore reading bits and piccces.

Files on a Unix system are more than just blobs of data. They have various metadata attached, which can be queried, and sometimes changed.

The `rename` system call is wrapped in the `os.rename` Python function. Since `rename` is atomic, this can help implement operations that require a certain state.

Note that the `os` module tends to be a slight shim over operating system calls. The discussion here is relevant to Unix-like systems: Linux, BSD-based systems, and, for the most part, macOS. It is worth keeping in mind, but it is not worth pointing out each place where you are making Unix-specific assumptions.

For example,

```python
with open("important.tmp", "w") as fout:
    fout.write("The horse raced past the barn")
    fout.write("fell.\n")
os.rename("important.tmp", "important")
```

This ensures that you do not accidentally misunderstand the sentence when reading an important file. If the code crashes in the middle, instead of believing that the horse raced past the barn, you get nothing from `important`. You only rename `important.tmp` to `important` at the end, after the last word has been written to the file.

A directory the most important example of a file that is not a blob in Unix. The `os.makedirs` function allows you to ensure a directory exists easily with

```python
os.makedirs(some_path, exists_ok=True)
```

This combines powerfully with the path operations from `os.path` to allow the safe creation of a nested file.

```python
def open_for_write(fname, mode=""):
    os.makedirs(os.path.dirname(fname), exists_ok=True)
    return open(fname, "w" + mode)
```

```python
with open_for_write("some/deep/nested/name/of/file.txt") as fp:
    fp.write("hello world")
```

This can come in useful, for example, when mirroring an existing file layout.

The `os.path` module has mostly string manipulation functions that assume strings are file names. The `dirname` function returns the directory name, so `os.path.dirname("a/b/c")` would return a/b. Similarly, the `basename` function returns the "file name," so `os.path.basename("a/b/c")` would return c. The inverse of both is the `os.path.join` function, which joins paths; `os.path.join("some", "long/and/winding", "path")` would return some/long/and/finding/path.

Another set of functions in the os.path module has a slightly higher-level abstraction for getting file metadata. It is important to note that these functions are often light wrappers around operating system functionality and *do not* try to hide operating system quirks. This means that operating system quirks can "leak" through the abstraction.

The biggest metadata is os.path.exists. Does the file exist? This comes in handy sometimes, though often-case it is better to write code in a way that is agnostic of file existence: file existence can have races. Subtler are the os.path.is... functions (isdir, isfile, islink, etc.), which can decide if a file name points to what you expect.

The os.path.get... functions get non-boolean metadata: access time, modification time, c-time (sometimes shortened to "creation time" but misleadingly is not the actual time of creation in a set of subtle circumstances, more accurately referred to as "i-node modification time"). getsize gets the size of the file.

The shutil module ("shell utilities") contains some higher-level operations. shutil.copy copies a file's contents as well as metadata. shutil.copyfile copies the contents only. shutil.rmtree is the equivalent of rm -r, while shutil.copytree is the equivalent of cp -r.

Finally, temporary files are often useful. Python's tempfile module produces temporary files which are secure and resistant to leaks. The most useful functionality is NamedTemporaryFile, which can be used as a context.

The following shows what a typical usage looks like.

```python
with NamedTemporaryFile() as fp:
    fp.write("line 1\n")
    fp.write("line 2\n")
    fp.flush()
    function_taking_file_name(fp.name)
```

Note that the fp.flush there is important. The file object caches write until closed. However, NamedTemporaryFile vanishes when closed. Explicitly flushing it is important before calling a function that reopens the file for reading.

4.2 Processes

The main module to deal with running subprocesses in Python is `subprocess`. It contains a high-level abstraction that matches the intuitive model most have when they think of "running commands," rather than the low-level model implemented in Unix, using `exec` and `fork`.

It is also a powerful alternative to calling the `os.system` function, which is problematic in several ways. For one, `os.system` spawns an *extra* process, the shell. This means that it depends on the shell, which on some weirder installations can differ from a more "exotic" system shell, like `ash` or `fish`. Finally, the shell *parses* the string, which means the string must be properly serialized. This is a hard task to do since the formal specification for the shell parser is long. Unfortunately, it is *not* hard to write something that works fine most of the time, so most bugs are subtle and break at the worst possible time. This sometimes even manifests as a security flaw.

While the `subprocess` module is not completely flexible, it is perfectly adequate for most needs. It is divided into high-level functions and a lower-level implementation level. The high-level functions, which should be used in most circumstances, are `check_call` and `check_output`. Among other benefits, they behave like running a shell with `-e` or `set err.` They immediately raise an exception if a command returns with a non-zero value.

The slightly lower level is Popen, which creates processes and allows fine-grained configuration of their inputs and outputs. Both `check_call` and `check_output` are implemented on top of Popen. Because of that, they share some semantics and arguments. The most important argument is `shell=True`, and it is most important in that it is almost always a bad idea to use it. When the argument is given, a string is expected and is passed to the shell to parse it.

Shell parsing rules are subtle and full of corner cases. If it is a constant command, there is no benefit there. You can translate the command to separate arguments in code. If it includes some input, it is almost impossible to reliably escape it in a way that makes it impossible to introduce an injection problem. On the other hand, without this, creating commands on the fly is reliable, even in the face of potentially hostile inputs.

The following, for example, adds a user to the docker group.

```python
subprocess.check_call(["usermod", "-G", "docker", "some-user"])
```

Using check_call means that if the command fails for some reason, such as the user not existing, this automatically raises an exception. This avoids a common failure mode, where scripts do not report accurate status.

It is straightforward to make it a function that takes a username.

```
def add_to_docker(username):
    subprocess.check_call(["usermod", "-G", "docker", username])
```

Note that this is safe to call even if the argument contains spaces, #, or other characters with special meaning. To tell which groups the current user is currently in, you can run groups.

```
groups = subprocess.check_output(["groups"]).split()
```

Again, this automatically raises an exception if the command fails. If it succeeds, you get the output as a string. There is no need to manually read and determine end conditions.

Both of these functions have common arguments. cwd allows running a command inside of a given directory. This matters for commands which look in their current directory.

```
sha = subprocess.check_output(
        ["git", "rev-parse", "HEAD"],
        cwd="src/some-project").decode("ascii").strip()
```

This gets the current git hash of the project, assuming the project is a git directory. If it is not, git rev-parse HEAD returns non-zero, and causes an exception to be raised.

Note that you had to decode the output since subprocess.check_output, like most functions in a subprocess, returns a *byte string*, not a Unicode string. In this case, rev-parse HEAD always returns a hexadecimal string, so you used the ascii codec. This fails on any non-ASCII characters.

There are some circumstances under which using high-level abstractions is impossible; for example, having to send standard input or read the output in chunks is not possible with them.

Popen runs a subprocess and allows fine-grained control of the inputs and outputs. While all things are possible, most things are not easy to do correctly. The shell pattern of writing long pipelines is unpleasant to implement, even more unpleasant to make sure there are no lingering deadlock conditions, and unnecessary.

If a short message into standard input is needed, the best way is to use the `communicate` method.

```
proc = Popen(["docker", "login", "--password-stdin"], stdin=PIPE)
out, err = proc.communicate(my_password + "\n")
```

If longer input is needed, having `communicate` buffer it all in-memory might be problematic. While it is possible to write to the process in chunks, doing it without potentially getting deadlocks is non-trivial. The best option is often to use a temporary file.

```
with tempfile.TemporaryFile() as fp:
    fp.write(contents)
    fp.write(of)
    fp.write(email)
    fp.flush()
    fp.seek(0)
    proc = Popen(["sendmail"], stdin=fp)
    result = proc.poll()
```

In fact, in this case, you can even use the `check_call` function.

```
with tempfile.TemporaryFile() as fp:
    fp.write(contents)
    fp.write(of)
    fp.write(email)
    fp.flush()
    fp.seek(0)
    check_call(["sendmail"], stdin=fp)
```

If you are used to running processes in a shell, you are probably used to long pipelines.

```
$ ls -l | sort | head -3 | awk '{print $3}'
```

As noted, it is a best practice in Python to avoid true command parallelism. In all the cases, you tried to finish one stage before reading from the next. In Python, `subprocess` is generally only used for calling out to external commands. You usually use Python's built-in processing abilities for pre-processing of inputs and post-processing of outputs. In the preceding case, you would use `sorted`, slices, and string manipulation to simulate the logic.

The commands for text and number processing are seldom useful in Python, which has a good in-memory model for doing such processing. The general case for calling commands in scripts is for things that manipulate data in a way that is either only documented as accessible by commands; for example, querying processes via `ps -ef`, or where the alternative to the command is a subtle library, sometimes requiring binary binding, such as in the case of `docker` or `git`.

This is one place where translating shell scripts into Python must be done with care and thought. Where the original had a long pipeline that depended on ad hoc string manipulation via `awk` or `sed`, Python code can be less parallel and more obvious. It is important to note that there is something lost in translation in those cases. The original low-memory requirements and transparent parallelism. However, in return, you get more maintainable and debuggable code.

4.3 Networking

Python has plenty of networking support. It has it from the lowest level—support of the `socket`-based system calls to high-level protocol supports. Some of the best approaches to problems are built-in libraries. For other problems, the best solution is a third-party library.

The most straightforward translation of low-level networking APIs is in the `socket` module. This module exposes the `socket` object.

The HTTP protocol is simple enough you can implement a simple client straight from the Python interactive command prompt.

```
>>> import socket, json, pprint
>>> s = socket.socket()
>>> s.connect(('httpbin.org', 80))
>>> s.send(b'GET /get HTTP/1.0\r\nHost: httpbin.org\r\n\r\n')
40
>>> res = s.recv(1024)
>>> pprint.pprint(json.loads(
...             res.decode('ascii').split('\r\n\r\n', 1)[1]))
```

```
{'args': {},
 'headers': {'Connection': 'close', 'Host': 'httpbin.org'},
 'origin': '73.162.254.113',
 'url': 'http://httpbin.org/get'}
```

The line s = socket.socket() creates a new socket *object*. There are various things that you can do with socket objects. One of them is to connect them to an endpoint; in this case, to the httpbin.org server on port 80. The default socket type is a *stream*, *Internet* type, which is the way Unix refers to TCP sockets.

After the socket is connected, you can send bytes to it. With sockets, only byte strings can be sent. You read back the result, do some ad hoc HTTP response parsing, and parse the actual content as JSON.

Generally, it is better to use a real HTTP client, but this showcases how to write low-level socket code. This can be useful, for example, if you want to diagnose a problem by replaying exact messages.

The socket API is subtle, and the example has a few incorrect assumptions. In most cases, this code works but fails in strange ways in the face of corner cases.

The send method is allowed to not send all the data if not all of it can fit into the internal kernel-level send buffer. This means that it can do a "partial send." It returned 40, which was the entire length of the byte string. Correct code checks for the return value and sends the remaining chunks until nothing is left. Luckily, Python already has a method to do it: sendall.

However, a more subtle problem occurs with recv. It returns as much as the kernel-level buffer has because it does not know how much the other side intended to send. Again, much of the time, especially for short messages, this works fine. For protocols like HTTP 1.0, the correct behavior is to read until the connection is closed.

Here is a fixed version of the code.

```
>>> import socket, json, pprint
>>> s = socket.socket()
>>> s.connect(('httpbin.org', 80))
>>> s.sendall(b'GET /get HTTP/1.0\r\nHost: httpbin.org\r\n\r\n')
>>> resp = b''
>>> while True:
...     more = s.recv(1024)
...     if more == b'':
```

```
...                break
...        resp += more
...
>>> pprint.pprint(json.loads(resp.decode('ascii').split('\r\n\r\n')[1]))
{'args': {},
 'headers': {'Connection': 'close', 'Host': 'httpbin.org'},
 'origin': '73.162.254.113',
 'url': 'http://httpbin.org/get'}
```

This is a common problem in networking code and can happen using higher-level abstractions. Things can appear to work in simple cases while failing in more extreme circumstances, such as high load or network congestion.

There are ways to test for these things. One of them is using proxies that exhibit extreme behaviors. Writing, or customizing proxies, requires low-level network coding using socket.

Python also has higher-level abstractions for networking. While the urllib and urllib2 modules are part of the standard library, best practices on the web evolve fast, and in general, for higher-level abstractions, third-party libraries are usually better.

One of the most popular is a third-party library, requests. With requests, getting a simple HTTP page is much simpler.

```
>>> import requests, pprint
>>> res=requests.get('http://httpbin.org/get')
>>> pprint.pprint(res.json())
{'args': {},
 'headers': {'Accept': '*/*',
             'Accept-Encoding': 'gzip, deflate',
             'Connection': 'close',
             'Host': 'httpbin.org',
             'User-Agent': 'python-requests/2.19.1'},
 'origin': '73.162.254.113',
 'url': 'http://httpbin.org/get'}
```

Instead of crafting your own HTTP requests out of raw bytes, all you needed to do was to give a URL similar to a URL you might type into a browser. Requests parsed it to find the host to connect to (`httpbin.org`), the port (80, the default for HTTP), and the path (`/get`). Once the response came in, it automatically parsed it into headers and content and allowed you to access the content directly as JSON.

As easy as `requests` are to use, it is almost better to put in more effort and use the `Session` object. Otherwise, the default session is used. This leads to code with non-local side effects: one sublibrary that calls requests changes a session state, which leads to another sublibrary's calls to act differently. For example, HTTP cookies are shared across a session.

The preceding code would be better written as follows.

```
>>> import requests, pprint
>>> session = requests.Session()
>>> res = session.get('http://httpbin.org/get')
>>> pprint.pprint(res.json())
{'args': {},
 'headers': {'Accept': '*/*',
             'Accept-Encoding': 'gzip, deflate',
             'Connection': 'close',
             'Host': 'httpbin.org',
             'User-Agent': 'python-requests/2.19.1'},
 'origin': '73.162.254.113',
 'url': 'http://httpbin.org/get'}
```

In this example, the request is simple, and the session state does not matter. However, this is a good habit; even in the interactive interpreter, avoid using the `get`, `put`, and other functions directly and use only the session interface.

It is natural to use an interactive environment to prototype code that would later make it into a production program. By keeping good habits like this, you ease the transition.

4.4 Summary

Python is a powerful tool for automating operating system operations. This comes from having libraries that are thin wrappers around native operating system calls and powerful third-party libraries.

This allows you to get close to the operating systems without any intervening abstractions and write high-level code that does not care about the details when these do not matter.

This combination often makes Python a superior alternative for writing scripts instead of the Unix shell. It does require a different way of thinking. Python is not as suitable for the long pipeline of text transformers approach, but in practice, those long pipelines of text transformers turn out to be an artifact of shell limitations.

With a modern memory-managed language, it is often easier to read the entire text stream into memory and then manipulate it without being limited to only those transformations specified as pipes.

CHAPTER 5

Testing

Too often, code used for automating systems does not have the same attention for testing as application code. DevOps teams are often small and under tight deadlines. Such code is also hard to test since it is meant to automate large systems, and proper isolation for testing is non-trivial.

However, testing is one of the best ways to increase code quality. It helps make code more maintainable in many ways. It also lowers defect rates. For code where defects can often mean total system outage since it often touches *all* the parts of the system, this is important.

5.1 Unit Testing

Unit tests serve several distinct purposes. It is important to keep these purposes in mind, as the resulting pressures on the unit tests are sometimes at odds.

The first purpose is as an API usage example. This is sometimes summarized with the somewhat-inaccurate term test-driven development and sometimes summarized with another somewhat-inaccurate term. The unit tests are the documentation.

Test-driven development means writing the unit tests before the logic, but it usually has little impact on the final source code commit, which contains both the unit tests and the logic, unless care is taken to preserve the original branch-wise commit history.

However, what does show up in the commit is the unit tests as ways to exercise the API. It is, ideally, not the only documentation of the API. However, it serves as a useful reference-of-last-resort; at the very least, you know that the unit tests call the API correctly and get the results they expect.

© Moshe Zadka 2022
M. Zadka, *DevOps in Python*, https://doi.org/10.1007/978-1-4842-7996-0_5

You also want to be confident that the logic expressed in the code does the right thing. This is often done with regression tests, which make sure that a bug detected by someone is truly fixed. However, since the code developer is aware of the potential edge-cases and trickier flows, they are often able to add that test *before* such a bug makes it out into the externally observed code change. However, such a confidence-increasing test looks exactly like a regression test.

A final reason is to avoid incorrect future changes. This is different from the regression test in that often, the case being tested is straightforward for the code as is, and other tests already cover the flows involved. However, some potential optimizations or other natural changes might break this case, so including it helps a future maintenance programmer.

When writing a test, it is important to think about which of those goals it is meant to accomplish. A good test accomplishes more than one.

All tests have two potential impacts.

- Make the code better by helping with future maintenance work

- Make the code worse by making future maintenance work harder

Every test does some of both. A good test does more of the first; a bad test does more of the second. One way to reduce the bad impact is to consider if the test is testing something that the code promises to do. If the answer is no, it is valid to change the code in some way that breaks the test but does not cause any bugs. This means the test must be changed or discarded.

When writing tests, it is important to test the actual contract of the code.

Here is an example.

```python
def write_numbers(fout):
    fout.write("1\n")
    fout.write("2\n")
    fout.write("3\n")
```

This function writes a few numbers into a file.

A bad test might look like this:

```python
class DummyFile:

    def __init__(self):
        self.written = []
```

```
def write(self,  thing):
    self.written.append(thing)
def test_write_numbers():
    fout = DummyFile()
    write_numbers(fout)
    assert  fout.written  ==  ["1\n",  "2\n",  "3\n"]
```

This is a bad test because it checks for a promise that write_numbers never made—that each write only writes one line.

A future refactor might look like this:

```
def write_numbers(fout):
    fout.write("1\n2\n3\n")
```

This keeps the code correct; all users of write_numbers still have correct files but cause a change in the test.

A slightly more sophisticated approach is to concatenate the strings written.

```
class DummyFile:
    def __init__(self):
        self.written = []

    def write(self, thing):
        self.written.append(thing)
def test_write_numbers():
    fout = DummyFile()
    write_numbers(fout)
    assert_that("".join(fout.written), is_("1\n2\n3\n"))
```

Note that this test works before and after the hypothetical optimization I suggested. However, this still tests more than the implied contract of write_numbers. After all, the function is supposed to operate on files; it might use another method to write.

The test would break if you modified write_numbers as follows.

```
def write_numbers(fout):
    fout.writelines(["1\n",
                     "2\n",
                     "3\n"]
```

A good test only breaks if there is a bug in the code. However, this code still works for the users of write_numbers, meaning that the maintenance now involved unbreaking a test, pure overhead.

Since the contract is to be able to write to file objects, it is best to supply a file object. In this case, Python has a ready-made one.

```
def test_write_numbers():
    fout = io.StringIO()
    write_numbers(fout)
    assert_that(fout.getvalue(), is_("1\n2\n3\n"))
```

In some cases, this requires writing a custom fake. The concept of fakes and how to write them is covered later.

You learned about the *implicit* contract of write_numbers. Since it had no documentation, you could not know the original programmer's intent. This is, unfortunately, common— especially in internal code only used by other pieces of the project. Of course, it is better to clearly document programmer intent. In the face of a lack of clear documentation, however, it is important to make *reasonable assumptions* about the implicit contract.

Earlier, the assert_that and is_ functions verified that the values were what you expected. Those functions come from the hamcrest library. This library, ported from Java, allows specifying properties of structures and checks that they are satisfied.

Using the pytest test runner to run unit tests makes it possible to use regular Python operators with the assert keyword and get useful test failures. However, this binds the tests to a specific runner and has a specific set of assertions that get treated, especially for useful error messages.

Hamcrest is an open-ended library. While it has built-in assertions for the usual things (equality, comparisons, sequence operations, and more), it also allows you to define specific assertions. Those come in handy when handling complicated data structures, such as those returned from APIs, or when only specific assertions can be guaranteed by the contract (for example, the first three characters can be arbitrary but must be repeated somewhere inside the string).

This allows you to test the *exact* contract of the function. It is another tool for avoiding over-testing; testing implementation details that can change, requiring changing the test when no real users have been broken. This is crucial for three reasons.

One is straightforward; time spent updating tests that could have been avoided is time wasted. DevOps teams are usually small, and there is little room to waste resources.

The second is that getting used to changing tests when they fail is a bad habit. When behavior has changed due to a bug, people assume that updating the test is the right thing to do.

Finally, and most importantly, combining those two lowers the return on investment on unit testing and, worse, the *perceived* return on investment. As a result, there is organizational pressure to spend less time writing tests. Bad tests that test implementation details are the single biggest cause for the meme that writing unit tests for DevOps code is not worth it.

For example, let's assume you have a function where all you can assert confidently is that the result has to be divisible by one of the arguments.

```python
from hamcrest.core import base_matcher

class DivisibleBy(base_matcher.BaseMatcher):

    def __init__(self, factor):
        self.factor = factor

    def _matches(self, item):
        return (item % self.factor) == 0

    def describe_to(self, description):
        description.append_text('number divisible by')
        description.append_text(repr(self.factor))

def divisible_by(num):
    return DivisibleBy(num)
```

This example uses pyhamcrest, a third-library package for writing test assertions. The package can be installed in a virtual environment using pip install pyhamcrest.

By convention, you wrap constructors in a function. This is usually useful if you want to convert the argument to a matcher, which in this case would not make sense.

```python
def test_scale():
    result = scale_one(3, 7)
    assert_that(result,
```

```
        any_of(divisible_by(3),
               divisible_by(7)))
```

You get an error like the following.

```
Expected: (number divisible by 3 or number divisible by 7)
     but: was <17>
```

It lets you test exactly what the contract of scale_one promises; in this case, it would scale up one of the arguments by an integer factor.

The emphasis on the importance of testing precise contracts is not accidental. This emphasis, which is a skill that is possible to learn and has principles that are possible to teach, makes unit tests into something that accelerates the process of writing code rather than making it slower.

Much of the reason people have an aversion to unit tests as something that wastes time for DevOps engineers and leads to a lot of poorly tested code that is foundational for business processes such as the deployment of software is this misconception. Properly applying principles of high-quality unit testing leads to a more reliable foundation for operational code.

5.2 Mocks, Stubs, and Fakes

Typical DevOps code has outsized effects on the operating environment. Indeed, this is almost the definition of good DevOps code. It replaces a significant amount of manual work. Testing DevOps code needs to be done carefully. You cannot simply spin up a few hundred virtual machines for each test run.

Automating operations means writing code that can significantly impact production systems if run haphazardly. When testing the code, it is worthwhile to have a few of these side effects as possible. Even if you have high-quality staging systems, sacrificing one every time a bug in operational code would lead to a lot of wasted time. It is important to remember that unit tests run on the worst code produced. The act of running them, and fixing bugs, means even code committed into feature branches is likelier to be in better condition.

Because of that, you often try to run unit tests against a fake system. It is important to classify what you mean by fake and how it impacts unit tests and code design. It is worthwhile thinking about how to test the code well before writing it.

Test doubles are the neutral term for things that substitute for the systems not under test. Fakes, mocks, and stubs usually have a more precise meaning, although, in casual conversation, they are used interchangeably.

The most authentic test double is a verified fake. A verified fake fully implements the system's interface not under test, though often simplified; perhaps less efficiently implemented, often without touching any external operating system. The verified refers to the fact that the fake has its *own* tests, verifying that it does indeed implement the interface.

An example of a verified fake in tests is using a memory-only SQLite database instead of a file-based one. Since SQLite has its own tests, this is a verified fake. You can be confident it behaves like a real SQLite database.

Below the verified fake is the fake. The fake implements an interface but often does it in a rudimentary form that the implementation is simple and not worth the effort to test.

For example, it is possible to create an object with the same interface as `subprocess.Popen`, but that never actually runs the process. Instead, it simulates a process that consumes all standard input, outputs some predetermined content into standard output, and exits with a predetermined code.

This object, if simple enough, might be a *stub*. A stub is a simple object that answers with predetermined data, always the same, holding almost no logic. This makes it easier to write, but it does make it constrained in what tests it can do.

An *inspector*, or a *spy*, is an object that attaches to a test double and monitors the calls. Often, part of the contract of a function is that it calls some method with specific values. An inspector records the calls and can be used in assertions to make sure the right calls get the right arguments.

You get a mock if you combine an inspect with a stub or a fake. Since this means that the stub/fake has more functionality than the original (at least, whatever is needed to check the recording), this can lead to some side effects. However, the simplicity and immediacy of creating mocks often compensate by making testing code simpler.

5.3 Testing Files

The filesystem is, in many ways, the most important thing about a Unix system. While the slogan everything is a file falls short of describing modern systems, the filesystem is still at the heart of most operations.

The filesystem has several properties that are worthwhile to consider when testing file manipulation code.

First, filesystems tend to be robust. While bugs in filesystems are not unknown, they are rare, far between, and usually only triggered by extreme conditions or an unlikely combination of conditions.

Next, filesystems tend to be fast. Consider that unpacking a source tarball, a routine operation, quickly creates many small files (several kilobytes). This is a combination of fast system call mechanisms and sophisticated cache semantics when reading or writing files.

Filesystems also have a curious fractal property; except for some esoteric operations, a sub-subdirectory supports the same semantics as the root directory.

Finally, filesystems have a very thick interface. Some of it is built into Python. Consider that the module system reads files directly. There are also third-party C libraries that use their internal wrappers to access the filesystem and several ways to open files even in Python, such as the built-in `file` object and the `os.open` low-level operations.

5.3.1 Testing with Subdirectories

For most file manipulation code, faking out or mocking the filesystem is a low return on investment. To make sure you are only testing the contract of a function, the investment is considerable since the function could switch to low-level file manipulation operations. You would need to reimplement a significant portion of Unix file semantics. The return is low. Using the filesystem directly is fast, reliable, and, as long as the code allows you to pass an alternative root path, almost side-effect free.

The best way to design file manipulation code is to allow passing in such a root path argument, even if the default is `/`. Given such design, the best way to test is to create a temporary directory, populate it appropriately, call the code, and garbage collect it.

If you create the temporary directory using Python's built-in `tempfile` module, you can configure the tox runner to put the temporary file inside of tox's built-in temporary directory. This keeps the general filesystem clean and is usually compatible with whatever version control the `ignore` file already uses to ignore tox artifacts.

```
[tox]
skipsdist = True
[testenv]
```

```
setenv =
    TMPDIR = {envtmpdir}
commands =
    python -c \
        'import os,sys;os.makedirs(sys.argv[1], exist_ok=True)' \
        {envtmpdir}
    # Rest of testing commands go here.
    python -c \
        'import os,sys;print(os.stat(sys.argv[1]))' \
        {envtmpdir}
```

Creating the temporary directory is important since Pythons `tempfile` only uses the environment variable when pointing to a real directory. Some versions of tox create the directory automatically, while others do not. It is best to ensure it exists to avoid unpleasant surprises.

As an example, you write tests for a function that looks for `.js` files and renames them as `.py`.

```
def javascript_to_python_1(dirname):
    for fname in os.listdir(dirname):
        if fname.endswith('.js'):
            os.rename(fname, fname[:-3] + '.py')
```

This function uses the `os.listdir` call to find the file names, and then renames them with `os.rename`.

```
def javascript_to_python_2(dirname):
    for fname in glob.glob(os.path.join(dirname, "*.js")):
        os.rename(fname, fname[:-3] + '.py')
```

This function uses the `glob.glob` function to filter by wildcard all the files that match the `*.js` pattern.

```
def javascript_to_python_3(dirname):
    for path in pathlib.Path(dirname).iterdir():
        if path.suffix == '.js':
            path.rename(path.parent.joinpath(path.stem + '.py'))
```

The function uses the built-in module `pathlib` (new in Python 3) to iterate on the directory and find its children. The real function under test is not sure which implementation to use.

```python
def javascript_to_python(dirname):
    return random.choice([javascript_to_python_1,
                          javascript_to_python_2,
                          javascript_to_python_3])(dirname)
```

Since you cannot be sure which *implementation* the function uses, you are left with only one choice: test the actual contract.

To write a test, you define some helper code. In a real project, this code lives in a dedicated module, possibly named something like `helpers_for_tests`. This module would be *tested* with its own unit tests.

You first create a context manager for the temporary directory. This ensures that the temporary directory is cleaned up.

```python
@contextlib.contextmanager
def get_temp_dir():
    temp_dir = tempfile.mkdtemp()
    try:
        yield temp_dir
    finally:
        shutil.rmtree(temp_dir)
```

Since this test needs to create many files, and you do not care about their contents, define a helper method.

```python
def touch(fname, content=''):
    with open(fname, 'a') as fpin:
        fpin.write(content)
```

Now with the help of these functions, you can finally write a test.

```python
def test_javascript_to_python_simple():
    with get_temp_dir() as temp_dir:
        touch(os.path.join(temp_dir, 'foo.js'))
        touch(os.path.join(temp_dir, 'bar.py'))
        touch(os.path.join(temp_dir, 'baz.txt'))
```

```
javascript_to_python(temp_dir)
assert_that(set(os.listdir(temp_dir)),
            is_({'foo.py', 'bar.py', 'baz.txt'}))
```

For a real project, you would write more tests, many of them possibly using the get_ temp_dir and touch helpers.

If you have a function that is supposed to check a specific path, you can have it take an argument to relativize its paths.

For example, let's say you want a function to analyze the Debian installation paths and give you a list of all domains you download packages from.

```python
def _analyze_debian_paths_from_file(fpin):
    for line in fpin:
        line = line.strip()
        if not line:
            continue
        line = line.split('#', 1)[0]
        parts = line.split()
        if parts[0] != 'deb':
            continue
        if parts[1][0] == '[':
            del parts[1]
        parsed = hyperlink.URL.from_text(parts[1].decode('ascii'))
        yield parsed.host
```

A naive approach would be to test _analyze_debian_paths_from_file. However, it is an internal function and has *no* contract. The implementation can change, perhaps reading the files and then scanning all strings, or possibly breaking up this function and letting the top level handle the line loop.

Instead, you want to test the public API.

```python
def analyze_debian_paths():
    for fname in os.listdir('/etc/apt/sources.list.d'):
        with open(os.path.join('/etc/apt/sources.list.d', fname)) as fpin:
            yield from _analyze_debian_paths_from_file(fpin)
```

However, you cannot control the /etc/apt/sources.list.d directory without root privileges. Even with root privileges, letting each test run control such a sensitive directory would be a risk. Additionally, many continuous integration systems are not designed for running tests with root privileges for good reasons, making this a problematic approach.

Instead, you can generalize the function a little bit, which means intentionally expanding the official, public API of the function to allow testing. This is definitely a trade-off.

However, the expansion is minimal. All you need is an explicit directory in which to work. In return, you get to simplify the testing requirements while avoiding any kind of patching, which inevitably starts poking at private implementation details.

```python
def analyze_debian_paths(relative_to='/'):
    sources_dir = os.path.join(relative_to, 'etc/apt/sources.list.d')
    for fname in os.listdir(sources_dir):
        with open(os.path.join(sources_dir, fname)) as fpin:
            yield from _analyze_debian_paths_from_file(fpin)
```

Now, using the same helpers as before, you can write a simple test for this.

```python
def test_analyze_debian_paths():
    with get_temp_dir() as root:
        touch(os.path.join(root, 'foo.list'),
              content='deb http://foo.example.com\n')
        ret = list(analyze_debian_paths(relative_to=root))
        assert(ret, equals_to(['foo.example.com']))
```

Again, in a real project, you would write more than one test and try to make sure many more cases are covered. Those could be built using the same techniques.

It is a good habit to add a relative_to parameter to any function that accesses specific paths.

5.3.2 Accelerating Tests with eatmydata

Unix operating systems try to be efficient with writes to disk. After data has been given to the OS to write, it tries to optimize when to write it to disk to minimize performance impact. This comes with a downside; some data might not be written to disk if the operating system crashes midstream.

Some applications cannot afford this risk. In these cases, there are ways to make sure the OS writes pending data to the disk. The name for this operation is sync (from synchronize).

There are a handful of system calls that expose sync-related functionality. The most common is fsync, wrapped by Pythons os module as os.fsync(). These system calls trade performance in favor of correctness. In general, this is a good trade-off to make. When running tests, however, if the OS crashes midstream, the test results are suspect anyway, and the tests need to run again.

Because of that, when *testing* code that uses os.fsync(), it would be nice to be able to turn this functionality off. The risk that the data being lost is worth it.

The libeatmydata library and the eatmydata executable are tools to turn off the sync functionality in programs. They are not Python-specific, which means that they help even if the sync is deep inside a C library that is linked to the code under test.

For eatmydata to show its value, the code must use fsync. The following is a code example.

```python
last = datetime.datetime.now()

with open("foo.txt", "w") as fpout:
    for i in range(1, 101):
        fpout.write("X")
        fpout.flush()
        os.fsync(fpout.fileno())
        if i % 10 == 0:
            current = datetime.datetime.now()
            print("Done", i, round((current-last).total_seconds(), 2))
            last = current
```

This code writes only a hundred bytes to a file. It does so extremely inefficiently. On a reasonably modern computer, the output might look like the following.

```
$ python write_stuff.py
Done 10 0.35
Done 20 0.34
Done 30 0.34
Done 40 0.34
Done 50 1.41
Done 60 0.34
Done 70 0.44
Done 80 0.46
Done 90 1.27
Done 100 0.46
```

Even in the best iterations, 10 bytes take more than a third of a second to write. As is typical for fsync(), this is not merely slow but variable. The worst iteration takes 1.41 seconds to write those ten bytes.

How much can eatmydata speed it up?

```
$ eatmydata python write_stuff.py Done 10 0.0
Done 20 0.0
Done 30 0.0
Done 40 0.0
Done 50 0.0
Done 60 0.0
Done 70 0.0
Done 80 0.0
Done 90 0.0
Done 100 0.0
```

It is so fast that the rounding rounds it down to 0. Without rounding, numbers look like 4.2e-05—over 8000 times faster.

Note that this code is intentionally worst-case for fsync(). In general, the speed-up is not as dramatic.

It is possible to useeatmydata as eatmydata tox when running the entire tox test suite. This requires all developers to remember to use it. It is even better if tox does it.

```
[testenv]
allowlist_externals  =  eatmydata
```

```
commands =
    eatmydata python write_stuff.py
```

Note that it is important to add eatmydata to allowlist_externals for this to work correctly.

At the time of writing, tox deprecates running commands outside of the virtual environment or explicitly allowed external commands. A future version will disable that completely.

Another way of enabling eatmydata from tox relies on understanding its internal mechanism.

The way fsync() is disabled relies on an interesting feature in how the OS runs programs. Most programs are dynamically linked. This means they get functions from the standard C library, like fsync(), by looking for them after they start, not at compile time.

When the LD_PRELOAD variable is set, the dynamic linker loads a dynamic library before loading the libraries that were originally linked against it. This means that a function in the library that LD_PRELOAD points at overrides those from any explicitly linked libraries, including the standard C library.

The eatmydata executable sets the LD_PRELOAD variable to libeatmydata.so and then runs the command. With the write configuration, tox can do the same and skip a layer of abstraction.

```
[testenv]
setenv =
    LD_PRELOAD = libeatmydata.so
commands =
    python write_stuff.py
```

This way of configuration can be useful in many places. For example, environment variables are easier to conditionally turn on or off depending on the environment. This allows some environments to run the command as is (maybe when eatmydata is not available) and lets others use it.

5.3.3 Accelerating Tests with tmpfs

tmpfs is an in-memory filesystem. In other words, when it is mounted, it does not have a backing hard-drive store. All files on a tmpfs are gone when the operating system reboots or crashes.

One way to mount tmpfs is by using containers. Many CI/CD systems either run the build and test steps in containers or can be configured to do so.

The exact steps to mount tmpfs into a container depend on how the containers are running. In Kubernetes, this is done by an emptyDir volume with emptyDir.medium set to Memory. When using Docker or nerdctl to run containers, this is done with the --tmpfs MOUNT_DIRECTORY argument.

Assume a container has a mounted tmpfs as /app/tmpdir. One way to accelerate any test that writes to files, but especially one that uses fsync() heavily, is to make sure the files are written inside /app/tmpdir.

To show how to do this, the preceding code needs to become slightly more sophisticated. The code always writes to a file named foo.txt in the current directory.

A more typical way of writing file handling code is to avoid hardcoding. Most code is written to accept file names as parameters. This code is similar to the preceding code, written as a function that accepts a file name.

```python
def write_to_file(fname):
    last = datetime.datetime.now()
    with open(fname, "w") as fpout:
        for i in range(1, 101):
            fpout.write("X")
            fpout.flush()
            os.fsync(fpout.fileno())
            if i % 10 == 0:
                current = datetime.datetime.now()
                print("Done", i, round((current-last).total_seconds(), 2))
                last = current
```

A typical way of testing such code is to use the tempfile module. This module creates temporary files, which is ideal for tests.

```python
def test_writer():
    with tempfile.NamedTemporaryFile() as fp:
```

```
        write_stuff.write_to_file(fp.name)
        data = fp.read()
    raise ValueError(len(data))
```

To have clearer output, this test is made to fail. The final raise in the last line allows the test output to be more thorough, as pytest adds debugging output.

Often tox.ini is written to force temporary files into the .tox directory. Even in cases where code catastrophically crashes since tox is cleaning the temporary directory between runs, this helps make sure there are no ugly leftovers.

```
[testenv]
deps = pytest
setenv =
    TEMP = {envtmpdir}
commands =
    pytest test_write_stuff.py
```

When running tox, this can take a while.

```
$ tox
...
test_write_stuff.py F                                           [100%]
================================ FAILURES ================================
_____ test_writer _____

    def test_writer():
        with tempfile.NamedTemporaryFile() as fp:
            write_stuff.write_to_file(fp.name)
            data = fp.read()
>       raise ValueError(len(data))
E       ValueError: 100

test_write_stuff.py:9: ValueError
-------------------------- Captured stdout call --------------------------
Done 10 0.54
Done 20 1.27
Done 30 0.5
Done 40 0.46
```

```
Done 50 1.34
Done 60 0.76
Done 70 0.56
Done 80 1.37
Done 90 0.59
Done 100 1.32
...
```

As expected, this fsync() heavy code takes a long time to write one hundred bytes.

If the tmpfs is mounted on /app/tmpdir, it is possible to force the tempfile module to use that. The trick is to know the order of the environment variables used in tempfile. The TMPDIR environment variable takes precedence.

```
$ TMPDIR=/app/tmpdir tox
...
test_write_stuff.py F                                              [100%]

================================ FAILURES ================================
_____ test_writer _____

    def test_writer():
        with tempfile.NamedTemporaryFile() as fp:
            write_stuff.write_to_file(fp.name)
            data = fp.read()
>       raise ValueError(len(data))
E       ValueError: 100

test_write_stuff.py:9: ValueError
-------------------------- Captured stdout call --------------------------
Done 10 0.0
Done 20 0.0
Done 30 0.0
Done 40 0.0
Done 50 0.0
Done 60 0.0
Done 70 0.0
Done 80 0.0
```

Done 90 0.0
Done 100 0.0
...

Even though the `fsync()` system call is not intercepted by a library like `eatmydata`, the speed rises dramatically. Since the `tmpfs` filesystem is memory-only, `fsync()` does nothing on it and takes little time.

5.4 Testing Processes

Testing process-manipulation code is often a subtle endeavor, full of trade-offs. In theory, the process of running code has a thick interface with the operating system. You learned about the `subprocess` module, but you can directly use the os.spawn* functions or the `os.fork` and `os.exec*` functions. Likewise, the standard output/input communication mechanism can be implemented in many ways, including using the Popen abstraction or directly manipulating file descriptors with `os.pipe` and `os.dup`.

Process-manipulation code can also be some of the most fragile. Running external commands depends on the behavior of those commands as a starting point. The interprocess communication means that the flow is inherently concurrent. It is too easy to make the tests rely on ordering assumptions that are not always true. Those mistakes can lead to flaky tests that pass most of the time but fail under seemingly random circumstances.

Those ordering assumptions can sometimes be true more often on development machines or unloaded machines, which means bugs only be exposed in production, or possibly in production only in extreme circumstances.

This is one of the reasons the chapter about using processes concentrated on ways to reduce concurrency and have things more sequential. It is worthwhile to carefully design process code to be reliably testable. Design often causes pressure on the code to be simple and reliable.

If the code only uses `subprocess.run` without taking advantage of exotic parameters, it is possible to use a simplified form of a pattern called dependency injection to make it testable. In this case, dependency injection is just a fancy way of saying passing parameters to a function. Consider the following function.

```
def error_lines(container_name):
    ret_value = subprocess.run(
```

```
    ["docker", "logs", container_name],
    capture_output=True,
    text=True,
    check=True,
)
for line in ret_value.stdout.splitlines():
    if 'error' in line:
        yield line
```

This function is unpleasant to test. Advanced patching can replace subprocess.run, but this would be error-prone and rely on implementation details. Instead, dependency injection explicitly elevates that implementation detail into being a part of the contract.

```
def error_lines(runner, container_name):
    ret_value = runner(
        ["docker", "logs", container_name],
    )
    for line in ret_value.stdout.splitlines():
        if 'error' in line:
            yield line
```

Now that runner is part of the official interface, testing becomes easier. This might seem a trivial change, but it is deeper than it looks. In some sense, error_lines has constrained its interface to process running.

The new version can be tested with unittest.mock.

```
def test_error_lines():
    runner = mock.MagicMock()
    runner.return_value.stdout = textwrap.dedent("""\
hello
error: 5 is not 6
goodbye
""")
    lines = list(error_lines(runner, "cool-container"))
    assert lines == ["error: 5 is not 6"]
    args, kwargs = runner.call_args
    assert kwargs == {}
```

```
assert len(args) == 1
[single_arg] = args
assert single_arg == ["docker", "logs", "cool-container"]
assert_that(lines, is_(["error: 5 is not 6"]))
```

The textwrap.dedent() function is useful in tests that need to create a multi-line string. This makes the code look nicer and indentation compatible without changing its values.

Note that this test does not restrict itself to *only* checking the contract. The code for error_lines could have run, for example, docker logs -- <container_name>.

This can slowly improve if the implementation does change until fidelity between the test and real life is achieved.

For example, the test can be modified to support -- as an argument separator.

```
def test_error_lines():
    runner = mock.MagicMock()
    runner.return_value.stdout = textwrap.dedent("""\
hello
error: 5 is not 6
goodbye
""")
    lines - list(error_lines(runner, "cool-container"))
    assert lines == ["error: 5 is not 6"]
    args, kwargs = runner.call_args
    assert kwargs == {}
    assert len(args) == 1
    [single_arg] = args
    command, rest = single_arg[:2], single_arg[2:]
    assert command == ["docker", "logs"]
    if rest[0] == "--":
        del rest[0]
assert rest == ["cool-container"]
```

This *still* works with the old version of the code and post-modification code. Fully emulating Docker is not realistic or worthwhile. However, this approach would slowly improve the accuracy of the test with no downsides.

If a significant amount of the code interfaces, for example, with Docker, there is often a mini-Docker emulator that can be factored out. Using higher-level abstractions for process running helps with this sort of approach.

Because processes are so hard to test, it is good to use process running only when necessary. Especially when porting over shell scripts to Python, often a good idea when they grow in complexity, it is good to substitute long pipelines with in-memory data processing.

Especially when factoring the code the right way, with the data processing as a simple, pure function that takes an argument and returns a value, the bulk of the code becomes much easier to test.

Imagine, for example, the following pipeline.

```
ps aux | grep conky | grep -v grep | awk '{print $2}' | xargs kill
```

This kills all processes that have conky in their names.

Here is a way to refactor the code to make it easier to test.

```python
def get_pids(lines):
    for line in lines:
        if 'conky' not in line:
            continue
        parts = line.split()
        pid_part = parts[1]
        pid = int(pid_part)
        yield pid

def ps_aux(runner):
    ret_value = runner(["ps", "aux"])
    return ret_value.stdout.splitlines()

def kill(pids, *, killer):
    for pid in pids:
        killer(pid, signal.SIGTERM)

def main():
    runner = functools.partial(
        subprocess.run,
        capture_output=True,
```

```
        text=True,
        check=True,
    )
    killer = os.kill
    kill(get_pid(ps_aux(runner)), killer=killer)
```

Note how the most complicated code is now in a pure function: get_pids. Hopefully, this means most bugs are there. Unit tests for get_pids can find those.

The code that is harder to unit test, ps_aux, has an ad hoc dependency injection. It is also simpler, so less testing is needed.

The main logic is in functions that do data processing. Testing those requires supplying data structures and observing the return value.

This *moves* potential bugs from the system-related code to *pure logic* code. The system-related code requires more effort to unit test than the pure logic code.

This does not *reduce* the bugs. It does move them to where they can be caught with unit tests. Writing these unit tests and making sure they pass *reduces the total number of bugs in a shipped version*.

With the input argument to subprocess.run, almost all process-manipulation code can be written like this.

For example, the following code makes a (potentially empty) commit and checks that the commit message is correct. It assumes it is running in a valid git directory.

```
def empty_hello_commit(runner):
    runner(
        ["git", "commit", "--allow-empty", "-F", "-"],
        input="hello world\n",
    )
    ret_value = runner(
        ["git", "log", "-n", "1"],
        capture_output=True,
    text=True,
        check=True,
    )
    lines = iter(ret_value.stdout.splitlines())
    for line in lines:
        if line == "":
```

```
            break
    if next(lines).strip() != "hello world":
        raise ValueError("commit failed", ret_value.stdout)
```

While it would have been easier to use git commit -m, this shows how to feed standard input into commands. In this case, git commit -F - expects a commit message on standard input.

The main code needs to initialize a runner.

```
runner = functools.partial(subprocess.run,
    capture_output=True,
    text=True,
    check=True,
)
empty_hello_commit(runner)
```

The empty_hello_commit function can be tested with similar techniques. It accepts a runner function as a parameter.

5.5 Testing Networking

When writing network code that deals with lower-level concepts, such as sockets, it is useful to write them in a test-friendly way. Since the creation of the socket object is separate from its usage, a lot of mileage can be gotten out of writing functions that accept socket objects and create them outside.

To simulate extreme conditions and see if the code can work despite them, you might want to write a dedicated class as a socket fake. To reduce boilerplate when writing the class, the following code uses the attrs library. This library can be installed in a virtual environment using pip install attrs.

```
import attr

@attr.s
class FakeSimpleSocket:

    _chunk_size = attr.ib()
```

```
_received = attr.ib(init=False, factory=list)

_to_send = attr.ib()

def connect(self, addr):
    pass

def send(self, blob):
    actually_sent = blob[:self._chunk_size]
    self._received.append(actually_sent)
    return len(actually_sent)

def recv(self, max_size):
    chunk_size = min(max_size, self._chunk_size)
    received, self._to_send = (self._to_send[:chunk_size],
                               self._to_send[chunk_size:])
    return received
```

This allows you to control the size of chunks. An extreme test would be to use a chunk_size of 1. This means bytes would go out one at a time and receive one at a time. No real network would be this bad, but a unit test allows you to simulate more extreme conditions than any reasonable network.

This fake is useful for testing networking code. For example, this code does some ad hoc HTTP to get a result.

```
import json

def get_get(sock):
    sock.connect(('httpbin.org', 80))
    sock.send(b'GET /get HTTP/1.0\r\nHost: httpbin.org\r\n\r\n')
    res = sock.recv(1024)
    return json.loads(res.decode('ascii').split('\r\n\r\n', 1)[1])

if __name__ == '__main__':
    # Sample code to exercise get_get
    import socket
    print(get_get(socket.socket()))
```

This code has a subtle bug in it. You can uncover the bug with a simple unit test using the socket fake.

```python
def test_get_get():
    result = dict(url='http://httpbin.org/get')
    headers = b'HTTP/1.0 200 OK\r\nContent-Type: application/json\r\n\r\n'
    output = headers + json.dumps(result).encode("ascii")
    fake_sock = FakeSimpleSocket(to_send=output, chunk_size=1)
    value = get_get(fake_sock)
    assert_that(value, is_(result))
```

This test would fail. The get_get assumes a good quality network connection, which simulates a bad one. The test would succeed if you changed chunk_size to 1024.

You could run the test in a loop, testing chunk sizes from 1 to 1024. In a real test, you would also check the sent data and send invalid results to see the response. The important thing is that none of those things need setting up clients or servers or trying to realistically simulate bad networks.

5.6 Testing HTTP Clients

Code that uses httpx as a web client can be made test-friendly by having most of it accept a httpx.Client as an argument. This is a good practice since it also allows adding support for complicated networking setups and configuring optimization parameters in one place.

A reductive example, using httpbin.org, can use the /put endpoint and the fact that it returns the data as the data parameter. The following code does not accomplish much, but it is an example of the skeleton of a function that accepts an httpx.Client as a parameter.

```python
def put_httpbin(client):
    resp = client.put("https://httpbin.org/put", json=dict(a=1, b=2))
    resp.raise_for_status()
    resp_value = resp.json()
    print("debug", resp_value)
    data = json.loads(resp_value["data"])
    return data["a"] + data["b"]
```

Assuming `httpbin.org` works correctly, it always returns 3. It is possible to write a naive test that runs it against the real `httpbin.org`.

```python
def test_put_httpbin_real():
    with httpx.Client() as client:
        value = put_httpbin(client)
    assert value == 4
```

This test fails since it compares the output to 4, not 3. Running this failing test with pytest shows the print output (`"debug"...`) in the function.

```
-------------------------- test_put_httpbin_real -------------------
---------

    def test_put_httpbin_real():
        with httpx.Client() as client:
            value = put_httpbin(client)
>       assert value == 4
E       assert 3 == 4

httpbin_httpx.py:36: AssertionError
-------------------------- Captured stdout call ---------------------------
debug {'args': {}, 'data': '{"a": 1, "b": 2}', ...
```

This test works correctly if the right value is used in the comparison. Running the tests against `httpbin.org` does come with its share of problems.

Some CI/CD environments limit communications with the outside Internet. The `httpbin.org` site might be down, causing tests to fail. Alternatively, running too many of these tests, perhaps due to a flurry of PRs, could lead to the endpoint denying the originating IP of the CI/CD system because of a sudden load spike.

One way to solve this is to use the fact that `httpx.Client` can run against in-process WSGI applications. Any Python web framework which can produce WSGI applications can be used to write local emulation.

The following code uses Pyramid to build minimal WSGI applications, which is enough to test the client.

```python
from pyramid import response, config

def return_put_data(request):
```

```
    data = request.body.decode("ascii")
    resp_value = json.dumps(dict(data=data)).encode("ascii")
    return response.Response(resp_value, content_type="application/json")

def make_app():
    with config.Configurator() as cfg:
        cfg.add_route('put', '/put')
        cfg.add_view(return_put_data, route_name='put')
        app = cfg.make_wsgi_app()
    return app
```

Notice that it is not a perfect emulation. It does not return the args or other fields that httpbin.org returns, only the data field.

This code makes it is possible to write a test that tests the client against the local emulation.

```
def test_put_httpbin_fake():
    with httpx.Client(app=make_app()) as client:
        value = put_httpbin(client)
    assert value == 4
```

This is the same as the ...._real test, except the parameter app is passed to the httpx.Client constructor. This parameter causes all HTTP calls that the client makes to be sent directly to the application.

This test causes the same failure as the real test.

```
-------------------------- test_put_httpbin_fake -------------------
---------

    def test_put_httpbin_fake():
        with httpx.Client(app=make_app()) as client:
            value = put_httpbin(client)
>       assert value == 4
E       assert 3 == 4

httpbin_httpx.py:30: AssertionError
-------------------------- Captured stdout call --------------------------
debug {'data': '{"a": 1, "b": 2}'}
```

Note that the debug output is different. This request has been made against the in-process WSGI application, not the real httpbin.org website.

This technique does require reconstructing a server version of any API the client uses. The implementation does not have to be complete, just enough to exercise the code and emulate any interesting edge-cases the real server has.

Because httpx.Client accepts any WSGI application, any Python web framework can be used to write the server emulation. Many Python web frameworks, including Flask, Pyramid, and Django, are popular and well-documented.

This makes writing such server emulations easier since both project-generated documentation and user-generated documentation are abundant. This expertise can be tapped for writing HTTP client tests, especially when working in a team that already uses Python web frameworks for a different reason.

CHAPTER 6

Text Manipulation

Automation of Unix-like systems often involves text manipulation. Many programs are configured with textual configuration files. Text is the output format and the input format of many systems.

Because of that, many automation tasks end up centering around text manipulation. While tools like sed, grep, and awk have their place, Python is a powerful tool for sophisticated text manipulation.

6.1 Bytes, Strings, and Unicode

When manipulating text or text-like streams, it is easy to write code that fails in funny ways when encountering a foreign name or emoji. These are no longer merely theoretical concerns; you have users from the entire world who insist on their usernames reflecting how they spell their names. You have people who write git commits with emojis in them. To make sure to write robust code which does not fail in ways that, to be fair, seem a lot *less* funny when they case a 3 a.m. page, it is important to understand that text is a subtle thing.

You can understand the distinction, or you can wake up at 3 a.m. when someone tries to log in with an emoji username.

Python 3 has two distinct types that represent the kind of things that are often in text files: bytes and strings. Bytes correspond to what RFCs usually refer to as octet-stream. This is a sequence of values that fit into 8 bits, or in other words, a sequence of numbers that are in the range 0 to 256 (including 0 and not including 256). When all these values are below 128, you call the sequence ASCII (American Standard Code of Information Interchange) and assign the meaning ASCII has assigned them to the numbers. When all these values are between 32 and 128 (including 32 and not including 128), you call the sequence printable ASCII or ASCII text. The first 32 characters are sometimes called *control characters*. The Ctrl key on keyboards is a reference to that; its original purpose was to be able to input those characters.

© Moshe Zadka 2022
M. Zadka, *DevOps in Python*, https://doi.org/10.1007/978-1-4842-7996-0_6

ASCII only encompasses the English alphabet used in America. To represent text in (almost) any language, there is Unicode. Unicode code points are (some of the) numbers between 0 and 2**32 (including 0 and not including 2**32). Each Unicode code point is assigned a meaning. Successive versions of the standards leave assigned meanings as is but add meanings to more numbers.

An example is the addition of more emojis. The International Standards Organization, ISO, ratifies versions of Unicode in its 10464 standard. For this reason, Unicode is sometimes called ISO-10464.

Unicode points that are also ASCII have the same meaning; if ASCII assigns a number uppercase A then so does Unicode.

Properly speaking, only Unicode is text, which Python strings represent. Converting bytes to strings or vice versa is done with an *encoding*. The most popular encoding these days is UTF-8. Confusingly, turning the bytes *to* text is decoding. Turning the text to bytes is encoding.

Remembering the difference between encoding and decoding is crucial to manipulate textual data. A way to remember it is that since UTF-8 *is* an encoding, moving from strings *to* UTF-8 encoded data is encoding while moving from UTF-8 encoded data to strings is decoding.

UTF-8 has an interesting property. When given a Unicode string that happens to be ASCII, it produces bytes with the values of the code points. This means that visually, the encoded and decoded form look the same.

```
>>> "hello".encode("utf-8")
b'hello'
>>> "hello".encode("utf-16")
b'\xff\xfeh\x00e\x00l\x00l\x00o\x00'
```

The example with UTF-16 shows that this is not a trivial property of encodings. Another property of UTF-8 is that if the bytes are *not* ASCII, and UTF-8 decoding of the bytes succeeds, it is unlikely that they were encoded with a different encoding. UTF-8 was designed to be *self-synchronizing*; starting at a random byte, it is possible to synchronize with the string with a limited number of bytes being checked. Self-synchronization was designed to allow recovery from truncation and corruption, but as a side benefit, it allows *detecting* invalid characters reliably and thus detects if the string was UTF-8.

This means trying decoding with UTF-8 is a safe operation. It does the right thing for ASCII-only texts. It works for UTF-8 encoded texts and fails cleanly for things that are neither ASCII nor UTF-8 encoded, either text in a different encoding or a binary format such as JPEG.

For Python, "fails cleanly" means throws an exception.

```
>>> snowman = '\N{snowman}'
>>> snowman.encode('utf-16').decode('utf-8')
Traceback (most recent call last):
  File "<stdin>", line 1, in <module>
UnicodeDecodeError: 'utf-8' codec can't decode byte 0xff in position 0:
invalid start ˍ
↪ byte
```

For random data, this also tends to fail.

```
>>> struct.pack('B'*12,
                *(random.randrange(0, 256)
                  for i in range(12))
).decode('utf-8')
```

The errors are random since the inputs are random. The following are some example errors.

```
UnicodeDecodeError: 'utf-8' codec can't decode byte 0xe2 in position 4:
invalid ˍ
↪continuation byte
UnicodeDecodeError: 'utf-8' codec can't decode byte 0x98 in position 2:
invalid start ˍ
↪byte
```

It is a good exercise to try and run this a few times; it rarely succeeds.

6.2 Strings

The Python string object is subtle. From one perspective, it appears to be a sequence of characters, and a *character* is a string of length 1.

```
>>> a="hello"
>>> for i, x in enumerate(a):
...     print(i, x, len(x))
...
0 h 1
1 e 1
2 l 1
3 l 1
4 o 1
```

The hello string has five elements, each of which is a string of length 1. Since the string is a sequence, the usual sequence operations work on it.

You can create a slice by specifying both endpoints.

```
>>> a[2:4]
'll'
```

Or, you can create a slice by specifying only the end.

```
>>> a[:2]
'he'
```

Or, you can create a slice by specifying only the beginning.

```
>>> a[3:]
'lo'
```

You can also use negative indices to count from the end.

```
>>> a[:-3]
'he'
```

You can reverse a string by specifying an extended slice with a negative step.

```
>>> a[::-1]
'olleh'
```

However, strings also have quite a few methods that are *not* part of the general sequence interface and are useful when analyzing text.

The startswith and endswith methods are useful since text analysis is often around the ends.

```
>>> "hello world".endswith("world")
True
```

A little-known feature is that endswith allows a tuple of strings and checks if it ends with any of these strings.

```
>>> "hello world".endswith(("universe", "world"))
True
```

An example where it comes in useful is testing for a few common endings.

```
>>> filename.endswith((".tgz",    ".tar.gz"))
```

You can easily test whether a file has either of the common suffixes for a gzipped tarball: the tgz or tar.gz suffix.

The strip and split methods are useful for parsing the ad hoc formats that many Unix files or utilities come in. For example, the /etc/fstab file contains static mounts on most Unix systems (though not on macOS-based ones).

```
with open("/etc/fstab") as fpin:
    for line in fpin:
        line = line.rstrip('\n')
        line = line.split('#', 1)[0]
        if not line:
            continue
        device, path, fstype, options, freq, passno = line.split()
        print(f"Mounting {device} on {path}")
```

This parses the file and prints a summary. The first line in the loop strips out the new line. The rstrip method strips from the right (the end) of the string.

Note that rstrip, as well as strip, accept a sequence of characters to remove. This means that passing a *string* to rstrip means any of the characters in the string and does *not* remove occurrences of this string. This does not affect one-character arguments to rstrip but does mean that longer strings are almost always a mistaken use.

You then remove comments, if any. You skip empty lines. For any line that is not empty, you use the split with no argument to split on any sequence of whitespaces. Conveniently, this convention is common to several formats, and the correct handling is built into the specification of split.

Finally, let's use a *format* string to format the output for easy consumption.

This is a typical usage of string parsing and is the kind of code that replaces long pipelines in the shell. Finally, the `join` method on a string uses glues together an iterable of strings.

A simple example of `' '.join(["hello", "world"])` returns `"hello world"`, but this only scratches the surface of `join`. Since it accepts an iterable, you can pass it anything that supports iteration.

```
>>> names=dict(hello=1,world=2)
>>> ' '.join(names)
'hello world'
```

Since iterating on a dictionary object yields the list of keys, passing it to join means you get a string with the list of keys joined together.

You can also pass in a generator.

```
>>> '-*-'.join(str(x) for x in range(3))
'0-*-1-*-2'
```

This allows calculating sequences on the fly and joining them without having intermediate storage for the sequence.

The usual question about `join` is why it is a method on the glue string rather than a method on sequences. The reason is exactly this. You can pass in an iterable, and the glue string glue in the bits in it.

Note that `join` does nothing to single-element iterables.

```
>>> '-*-'.join(str(x) for x in range(1))
'0'
```

6.3 Regular Expressions

Regular expressions are a special DSL for specifying properties of strings, also called patterns. They are common in many utilities, although each implementation has its own idiosyncrasies. In Python, regular expressions are implemented by the `re` module. It fundamentally allows two modes of interaction, one where regular expressions are auto-parsed at the time of text analysis and one where they are parsed in advance.

In general, the latter style is preferred. Auto-parsing the regular expression is suited only to an interactive loop, where they are used quickly and forgotten. For this reason, this usage is covered here.

To *compile* a regular expression, you use re.compile. This function returns a regular expression object that looks for strings that match the expression. The object can do several things; for example, find one match, find all matches, or even replace the matches.

The regular expression mini-language has a lot of subtlety. Here, only the basics needed to illustrate how to use regular expressions effectively are covered.

Most characters stand for themselves. The regular expression hello, for example, matches exactly hello. The . stands for any character. So hell. matches hello and hella, but not hell since the latter does not have any character corresponding to the .. Square brackets delimit character classes; for example, wom[ae]n matches both women and woman. Character classes can also have ranges in them: [0-9] matches any digit, [a-z] matches any lowercase character, and [0-9a-fA-F] matches any hexadecimal digit (hexadecimal digits and numbers pop up a lot in many places since two hexadecimal digits correspond exactly to a standard byte).

There are also repeat modifiers that modify the expression that precedes them. For example, ba?b matches both bb and bab, and the ? stands for zero or one. The * stands for any number, so ba*b stands for bb, bab, baab, baaab, and so on. If you want at least one, ba+b match almost everything that ba*b matches, except for bb. Finally, there are the exact counters: ba{3}b matches baaab while ba{1,2}b matches bab and baab and nothing else.

To make a special character (like . or *) match itself, prefix it with a backslash. Since the backslash has other meanings in Python strings, Python supports raw strings. While you can use any string to denote a regular expression; often, raw strings are easier.

For example, if you want a DOS-like file name regular expression: r"[^.]{1,8}\.[^.]{0,3}". This match, say, readme.txt but not archive.tar.gz. Note that to match a literal ., you must escape it with a backslash. Also note an interesting character class, [^.], which means anything except .. The ^ means exclude the inside of a character class.

Regular expressions also support *grouping*. Grouping does two things. It allows addressing parts of the expression and treating a part of the expression as a single object to apply one of the repeat operations to it. If only the latter is needed, this is a non-capture group, denoted by (?:....).

For example, (?:[a-z]{2,5}-){1,4}[0-9] matches hello-3 or hello-world-5 but not a-hello-2 (since the first part is not two characters long) or hello-world-this-is-too-long-7 since it is made up of six repetitions of the inner pattern, and you specified a maximum of 4.

This allows arbitrary nesting. To illustrate, (?:(?:[a-z]{2,5}-){1,4}[0-9];)+ allows any semi-colon-terminated separated sequence of the previous pattern; for example, az-2;hello-world-5; matches but this-is-3; not-good-match-6 does not since it is missing the ; at the end.

This is a good example of how complex regular expressions can get. It is easy to use this dense mini-language inside Python to specify constraints on strings that are hard to understand.

Once you have a regular expression object, there are two main methods in it: match and search. The match method looks for matches at the beginning of the string, while search looks for the first match, wherever it may start. When they find a match, they return a match object.

```
>>> reobj  =  re.compile('ab+a')
>>> m  = reobj.search('hello abba world')
>>> m
<_sre.SRE_Match object; span=(6, 10), match='abba'>
>>>  m.group()
'abba'
```

The first method that is often used is .group(), which returns the part of the string matched. This method can get a part of the match if the regular expression contains *capturing* groups. A capturing group is usually marked with ().

```
>>> reobj = re.compile('(a)(b+)(a)')
>>> m  = reobj.search('hello abba world')
>>> m.group()
'abba'
>>> m.group(1)
'a'
>>> m.group(2)
'bb'
>>> m.group(3)
'a'
```

When the number of groups is significant, or when modifying the group, managing the indices to the group can prove to be a challenge. If analysis of the groups is needed, you can also *name* the groups.

```
>>> reobj  =  re.compile('(?P<prefix>a)(?P<body>b+)(?P<suffix>a)')
>>> m  = reobj.search('hello abba world')
>>> m.group('prefix')
'a'
>>> m.group('body')
'bb'
>>> m.group('suffix')
'a'
```

Since regular expressions can get dense, there is a way to make them a bit easier to read: the verbose mode.

```
>>> reobj = re.compile(r"""
... (?P<prefix>a) # The beginning -- always an a
... (?P<body>b+)  # The middle -- any numbers of b, for emphasis
... (?P<suffix>a) # An a at the end to properly anchor
... """, re.VERBOSE)
>>> m = reobj.search("hello abba world")
>>> m.groups()
('a', 'bb', 'a')
>>> m.group('prefix'), m.group('body'), m.group('suffix')
('a', 'bb', 'a')
```

When compiling regular expressions with the re.VERBOSE flag allows making regular expressions more readable. Whitespace inside the regular expression is ignored. Additionally, Python-like comments (from "#" to the end of the line) are ignored. In order to match a space or #, those characters need to be escaped with a backslash.

This allows you to write long regular expressions while still making them easier to understand with judicious line breaks, spaces, and comments.

Regular expressions are loosely based on the mathematical theory of finite automaton. While they *do* go beyond the constraints of what finite automata can match, they are not fully general. They are poorly suited for *nested* patterns, whether matching parentheses or HTML elements is not a good fit for regular expressions.

6.4 JSON

JSON is a hierarchical file format that is simple to parse and reasonably easy to read and write by hand. It has its origins on the web and stands for JavaScript Object Notation. Indeed, it is still popular on the Internet; one reason to care about JSON is that many web APIs use JSON as a transfer format.

It is also useful, however, in other places. For example, in JavaScript projects, `package.json` includes the dependencies of this project. Parsing this is often useful to determine third-party dependencies for security or compliance audits.

In theory, JSON is a format defined in *Unicode*, not *bytes*. When serializing, it takes a data structure and transforms it into a Unicode string, and when deserializing, it takes a Unicode string and returns a data structure. However, the standard was recently amended to specify a preferred encoding: `utf-8`. With this addition, the format is also defined as a byte stream.

However, note that the encoding is still separate from the format in some use cases. In particular, when sending or receiving JSON over HTTP, the HTTP encoding is the ultimate truth. Even then, though, when no encoding is explicitly specified, UTF-8 should be assumed.

JSON is a simple serialization format, only supporting a few types.

- Strings

- Numbers

- Booleans

- A `null` type

- Arrays of JSON values

- Objects: dictionaries mapping strings to JSON values

Note that JSON does not fully specify numerical ranges or precision. If precise integers are required, the range $-2**53$ to $2**53$ can usually be assumed to be representable precisely.

Although the Python JSON library can read/write directly to files, you almost always separate the tasks; you read as much data as you need and pass the string directly to JSON.

The most important functions in the `json` module are `loads` and `dumps`. The `s` at the end stands for string, which is what those functions accept and return.

```
>>> thing = [{"hello": 1, "world": 2}, None, True]
>>> json.dumps(thing)
'[{"hello": 1, "world": 2}, null, true]'
>>> json.loads(_)
[{'hello': 1, 'world': 2}, None, True]
```

The None object in Python maps to the JSON null object, booleans in Python map to booleans in JSON, and numbers and strings map to number and strings. Note that the Python JSON parsing libraries make ad hoc decisions about whether a number should map to an integer or a float based on its notation.

```
>>>   json.loads("1")
1
>>>   json.loads("1.0")
1.0
```

It is important to remember not all JSON loading libraries make the same decision, and in some cases, this can lead to interoperability problems.

For debugging reasons, it is often useful to be able to print JSON. The dumps function can do that with some extra arguments. The following is the usual set of arguments for pretty printing.

```
json.dumps(thing,  indent-4)
```

If you want to round trip into an equivalent but prettier version, you can do so.

```
>>> encoded_string='{"b":1,"a":2}'
>>> print(json.dumps(json.loads(encoded_string), indent=4))
{
    "b": 1,
    "a": 2
}
```

Note that some code also adds sort_keys=True, which was a good idea on versions of Python prior to 3.5. Now, Python dictionaries are sorted by key insertions, which means that json.loads and json.dumps preserve the original order of the keys in the source JSON.

Finally, at the command line, the `json.tool` module does this automatically.

```
$ python -m json.tool < somefile.json | less
```

This is an easy way to scan through dumped JSON and look for interesting information.

One frequently missed type from JSON is a date-time type. Usually, this is represented with strings and is the most common need for a schema to parse JSON against to know which strings to convert to a `datetime` object.

6.5 CSV

The CSV format has a few advantages. It is constrained; it always represents scalar types in a two-dimensional array. For this reason, there are not a lot of surprises that can go in. In addition, it is a format that imports natively into spreadsheet applications like Microsoft Excel or Google Sheets, which comes in handy when preparing reports.

Examples of such reports are breaking down expenses for paying for third-party services for the financial department or a report on incidents managed and time to recovery for management. In all these cases, having a format that is easy to produce and import into spreadsheet applications allows for easy automation of the task.

Writing CSV files is done with `csv.writer`. A typical example involves serializing a homogenous array—an array of things with the same type.

```python
@attr.s(frozen=True, auto_attribs=True)
class LoginAttempt:
    username: str
    time_stamp: int
    success: bool
```

This class represents a login attempt by some user at a given time and with a record of the attempt's success. For a security audit, you need to send the auditors an Excel file of the login attempts.

```python
def write_attempts(attempts, fname):
    with open(fname, 'w') as fpout:
        writer = csv.writer(fpout)
        writer.writerow(['Username', 'Timestamp', 'Success'])
```

```
for attempt in attempts:
    writer.writerow([
        attempt.username,
        attempt.time_stamp,
        str(attempt.success),
    ])
```

Note that by convention, the first row should be a title row. Though the Python API does not enforce it, it is highly recommended to follow this convention. In this example, you first wrote a title row with the names of the fields.

Then you looped through the attempts. Note that CSV can only represent strings and numbers, so instead of relying on thinly documented standards on how a boolean is written, you do so explicitly.

This way, if the auditor asks for that field to be yes/no, you can change the explicit serialization step to match. When it comes to reading CSV files, there are two main approaches.

Using csv.reader returns an iterator that yields parsed row by parsed row as a list. However, assuming the convention about the first row being the names of fields has been followed, csv.DictReader yields nothing for the first row and a *dictionary* for every subsequent row, using field names as keys. This enables more robust parsing in the face of end-users adding fields or changing their order.

```
>>> fileobj = open("data.csv")
>>> reader = csv.DictReader(fileobj)
>>> list(reader)
[OrderedDict([('Username', 'alice'),
             ('Timestamp', '1514793600.0'),
             ('Success', 'False')]),
 OrderedDict([('Username', 'bob'),
             ('Timestamp', '1539154800.0'),
             ('Success', 'True')])]
```

Reading the same CSV you have written in the previous example yield reasonable results. The dictionary maps the field names to the values. It is important to note that the types have all been forgotten, and everything is returned as a string. Unfortunately, CSV does not keep type information.

It is sometimes tempting to just improvise parsing CSV files with `.split`. However, CSV has quite a few corner cases that are not readily apparent.

For example,

```
1,"Miami, FL","he""llo"
```

is properly parsed as

```
('1', 'Miami, FL', 'he"llo')
```

For the same reason, it is a good idea to avoid writing CSV files using anything other than `csv.writer`.

6.6 Summary

Much of the content needed for many DevOps tasks arrives as text: logs, JSON dumps of data structures, or a CSV file of paid licenses. Understanding what text is and how to manipulate it in Python allows much of the automation that is the cornerstone of DevOps, be it through build automation, monitoring result analysis, or just preparing summaries for easy consumption by others.

CHAPTER 7

HTTPX

Many systems expose a web-based API. The httpx library is useful for automating web-based APIs. It is designed to be easy to use while still exposing many powerful features.

Note that httpx does not support Python 2. If this is a concern, there are alternatives. It is important to remember that Python 2 is not getting security updates, so it is dangerous to use with a library designed to connect to websites.

Using httpx is almost always better than using Pythons standard library HTTP client facilities. It supports flexible authentication, internally serializes and deserializes JSON, and supports both synchronous and asynchronous operation.

Note that httpx is largely compatible with the popular requests library. Unless special features in requests are used, like exotic certificate validation, converting code that uses requests to use httpx mostly changes the import statements.

7.1 Clients

It is better to work with explicit clients in httpx. It is important to remember that there is no such thing as working *without* a client in httpx. When working with the functions, it uses the global client object.

This is problematic for several reasons. For one, this is exactly the kind of global mutable shared state that can cause hard-to-diagnose bugs. For example, when connecting to a website that uses cookies, another user of httpx connecting to the same website could override the cookies. This leads to subtle interactions between potentially far-apart pieces of code.

It is also problematic because this makes code non-trivial to unit tests. The httpx. get/httpx.post functions must be explicitly mocked. In contrast, httpx allows some interesting ways to fake explicit clients.

111

© Moshe Zadka 2022
M. Zadka, *DevOps in Python*, https://doi.org/10.1007/978-1-4842-7996-0_7

Last but not least, some functionality is only accessible when using an explicit Client object. If the requirement to use it comes later, for example, because you want to add a tracing header or a custom user-agent to all requests, refactoring all code to use explicit clients can be non-trivial.

It is much better for any code that expects to be long-lived to use an explicit client object. For similar reasons, it is even better to make most of this code not construct its own Client object but rather get it as an argument.

This allows initializing the client elsewhere, closer to the main code. It is useful because decisions about which proxies to use and when can happen closer to the end-user requirements rather than in abstract library code.

A client object is constructed with httpx.Client(). After that, the only interaction should be with the object. The client object has all the HTTP methods: .get(), .put(), .post(), .patch(), and .options().

Clients can be used as contexts.

```
with httpx.Client() as c:
    c.get(...)
```

At the end of the context, all pending connections are cleaned up, which is important, especially if a web server has strict usage limits that you cannot afford to exceed.

Note that counting on Pythons reference counting to close the connections can be dangerous. Not only is that not guaranteed by the language (and is not true, for example, in PyPy), but small things can easily prevent this. For example, the client can be captured as a local variable in a stack trace, and that stack trace can be involved in a circular data structure. This means that the connections are not closed for a potentially long time—not until Python does a circular garbage collection cycle.

The client supports a few constructor parameters you can set to send all requests in a specific way. The most common one to use is auth=. httpx authentication capabilities are further discussed later.

Another parameter that is useful to set is headers=. Those are the default headers that are sent with every request. This can sometimes be useful for the User-Agent variable.

When using httpx for testing your web APIs, it is useful to have an identifying string in the agent. This allows you to check the server logs and distinguish which requests came from tests instead of real users.

```
client = httpx.Client(
    headers={'User-Agent': 'Python/MySoftware ' + __version__ }
)
```

This lets you check which version of the test code caused a problem, especially if the test code crashes the server and you want to disable it, which can be invaluable in diagnosis.

The client also holds a `CookieJar` in the `.cookies.jar` member. The cookie jar can be explicitly set using a `Client(cookies=cookie_jar)` constructor parameter.

You can use it to persist cookies to disk and recover them if you want to have restartable HTTP sessions.

Finally, the client can have a client-side certificate in situations where this kind of authentication is desired. This can either be a `pem` file (the key and the certificate concatenated) or a tuple with the paths to the certificate and key file.

7.2 REST

REST stands for REpresentational State Transfer. It is a loose and loosely applied standard of representing information on the web. It is often used to map a row-oriented database structure almost directly to the web. When used this way, it is often called the CRUD model (create, retrieve, update, and delete). When using REST for CRUD, these web operations are often used.

You can create maps to `POST`, accessed via the `.post()` method on `httpx.Client`. In some sense, although the first on the list, it is the least RESTful of the four because its semantics are not replay safe. This means that if the `.post()` call raises a network-level error, for example, `socket.error`, it is not obvious how to proceed. Was the object created? If one of the fields in the object must be unique, for example, an email address for a user, then replaying is safe; it fails if the creation operation succeeded earlier.

However, this depends on *application* semantics, which makes it impossible to replay generically.

Luckily, the HTTP methods typically used for the other operations *are* replay safe. This property is also known as idempotency, inspired by (though not identical with) the mathematical notion of idempotent functions. If a network failure occurs, sending the operation again is safe.

If the server follows correct HTTP semantics, all operations that follow are replay safe.

The update operation is usually implemented with PUT (for a whole-object update) or PATCH (when changing specific fields).

The delete operation is implemented with HTTP DELETE. The replay safety here is subtle; whether a replay succeeds or fails with an object not found, in the end, you are left in a known state.

The retrieve operation, implemented with HTTP GET, is almost always read-only, and so it is replay safe, or safe to retry after a network failure.

Most REST services, nowadays, use JSON as the state representation. The httpx library has special support for JSON.

```
>>> from pprint import pprint
>>> pprint(c.get("https://httpbin.org/json").json())
{'slideshow': {'author': 'Yours Truly',
              'date': 'date of publication',
              'slides': [{'title': 'Wake up to WonderWidgets!',
              'type': 'all'},
                        {'items': ['Why <em>WonderWidgets</em>
                        are great',
                                  'Who <em>buys</em> WonderWidgets'],
                          'title': 'Overview',
                          'type': 'all'}],
              'title': 'Sample Slide Show'}}
```

The pprint built-in module allows printing with indentation and line breaks that are easier to read than print. The name stands for pretty print.

The return value from a request, Response, has a .json() method, which assumes the return value is JSON and parses it. While this only saves one step, it is a useful step to save in a multi-stage process where you get some JSON-encoded response only to use it in a further request.

It is also possible to auto-encode the request body as JSON.

```
>>> resp = c.put("https://httpbin.org/put", json=dict(hello=5,world=2))
>>> resp.json()['json']
{'hello': 5, 'world': 2}
```

The combination of those two, with a multi-step process, is often useful.

```
>>> res = c.get("https://api.github.com/repos/python/cpython/pulls")
>>> commits_url = res.json()[0]['commits_url']
>>> commits = c.get(commits_url).json()
>>> commits[0]['commit']['message'][:40]
'bpo-46104: Fix example broken by GH-3014'
```

This example of getting a commit message from the first pull request on the CPython project is a typical use of a good REST API. A good REST API includes *URLs* as resource identifiers. You can pass those URLs to a further request to get more information.

7.3 Security

The HTTP security model relies on *certification authorities*, often shortened to CAs. Certification authorities cryptographically sign public keys as belonging to a specific domain (or, less commonly, IP). To enable key rotation and revocation, certificate authorities do not sign the public key with their *root key* (the one trusted by the browser). Rather, they sign a signing key, which signs the public key. These chains, where each key signs the next one until the ultimate key is the one the server is using, can get long; often, there is a three or four-level deep chain.

Since certificates sign the *domain*, and often domains are co-hosted on the same IP, the protocol that requests the certificate includes Server Name Indication, or SNI. SNI sends the server name—unencrypted—that the client wants to connect to. Then the server responds with the appropriate certificate and proves that it owns the private key corresponding to the signed public key using cryptography.

Finally, optionally the client can engage in a cryptographic proof of its own identities, which is done through the slightly- misnamed client-side certificates. The client-side has to be initialized with a certificate *and* a private key. Then the client sends the certificate, and if the server trusts the certifying authority, it proves that it owns the corresponding private key.

Client-side certificates are seldom used in browsers but can sometimes be used by programs. For a program, they are usually *easier* secrets to deploy. Most clients, httpx included, support reading them out of files already. This makes it possible to deploy them using systems that make secrets available via files, like Kubernetes secrets or vault. It also means it is possible to manage permissions on them via normal Unix system permissions.

Usually, client-side certificates are not owned by a public CA. Rather, the server owner operates a *local* CA, which through some locally-determined procedure, signs certificates for clients. It can be anything from an IT person signing manually to a single sign-on (SSO) portal that auto-signs certificates.

To authenticate *server-side* certificates, httpx needs to have a source of client-side root CAs to accomplish secure connections. Depending on the subtleties of the ssl build process, it might or might not have access to the *system* certificate store.

The best way to have a good set of root CAs is to install the certifi package. This package has Mozilla-compatible certificates. Since httpx depends on certifi, it is already installed.

This is useful when making connections to the Internet; almost all sites are tested to work with Firefox and have a compatible certificate chain. If the certificate fails to validate, the error CERTIFICATE VALIDATE FAILED is thrown.

There is a lot of unfortunate advice on the Internet, including in httpx documentation, about the solution of passing in the verify=False flag, which is usually not good advice. Its usage violates the core assumption of TLS; the connection is encrypted and tamper-proof. For example, having a verify=False on the request means that any cookies or authentication credentials can now be intercepted by anyone who can modify in-stream packets, which is unfortunately common. ISPs and open access points often have operators with nefarious motivations.

Sometimes this would make sense in local testing of servers running self-signed certificates. However, even in those cases, the risk exists that code with verify=False is reused or repurposed for a different case without careful vetting.

A better alternative is to make sure that the correct certificates exist on the file system and pass the path to the verify argument via verify='/full/path/cert.pem'. At the very least, this allows you a form of trust on first use; manually get the certificate from the service, and bake it into the code. It is even better to attempt some out-of-band verification, for example, by asking someone to log in to the server and verify the certificate.

Choosing which SSL versions to allow or ciphers to allow is slightly more subtle. Again, there are a few reasons to do it. httpx is set up with good, secure defaults. However, sometimes there are overriding concerns; for example, avoiding a specific SSL version for regulatory reasons or testing purposes.

This can be done by customizing the SSL context.

```
import httpx
import ssl

ssl_context = ssl.create_default_context()
ssl_context.options |= ssl.OP_NO_TLSv1_3
client = httpx.Client(verify=ssl_context)
```

Since the client accepts an `ssl.SSLContext` object, you can customize it in any way the Python `ssl` allows. For example, `ssl_context.set_ciphers("RSA+AES")` only allows that specific cipher.

HTTPX also supports client-side certificates. Seldom used for user-to-service communication but sometimes used in microservice architectures, client-side certificates identify the client using the same mechanism servers identify themselves using cryptographically signed proofs. The client needs a private key and a corresponding certificate. These certificates are often signed by a private CA, which is part of the local infrastructure.

The certificate and the key can be concatenated into the same file, often called a PEM file. In that case, initializing the session to identify with it is done via

```
client = httpx.Client(cert="/path/to/pem/file.pem")
```

If the certificate and the private key are in separate files, they are given as a tuple.

```
client = httpx.Client(
    cert=("/path/to/client.cert", "/path/to/client.key")
)
```

Such key files must be carefully managed; anyone who has read access to them can pretend to be the client.

7.4 Authentication

The `auth=` keyword parameter to `httpx.Client()` configures the default authentication. Alternatively, `auth=` can be sent when making a request, using `.get()`, `.post()`, or one of the other request methods.

The most commonly used authentication is *basic auth*. The auth= argument can be a tuple (username, password). However, a better practice is to use an httpx.BasicAuth instance. This documents intent better and makes it easier to switch to other authentication forms.

It is also possible to implement your own authentication flow, which is done by subclassing httpx.Auth.

For simpler cases, it is enough to override auth_flow(), which is usually implemented as a *generator*. It accepts one parameter.

```
class MyAuth(httpx.Auth):

    def auth_flow(self, request: httpx.Request):
        ....
```

This method often modifies the request and then yields it, which is enough for authentication that can be done by setting headers, for example.

However, in more complicated flows, there may be more back-and-forth before authenticating to the server. For example, suppose that a server needs a user/password request against a login URL. In that case, for the response to return a cookie that can be used with subsequent calls, it is possible to yield the request to the login URL, capture the cookie, and then modify the request before sending it.

As a concrete example for a simple flow, the following is useful as an object that signs AWS requests with the V4 signing protocol.

The first thing you do is make the URL canonical. Canonicalization is the first step in many signing protocols. Since often higher levels of the software have already parsed the content by the time the signature checker looks at it, you convert the signed data into a standard form that uniquely corresponds to the parsed version.

The most subtle part is the query part. You parse it and re-encode it using the built-in urrlib.parse library.

```
from urllib.parse import parse_qs, urlencode

def canonical_query_string(query):
    if not query:
        return ""
    parsed = parse_qs(url.query, keep_blank_values=True)
    return "?" + urlencode(parsed, doseq=True)
```

You use this function in the URL canonicalization function.

```python
def to_canonical_url(raw_url):
    url = urlparse(raw_url)
    path = url.path or "/"
    query = canonical_query_string(url.query)
    return (
        url.scheme +
        "://" +
        url.netloc +
        path +
        query
    )
```

Let's make sure the path is canonical. You translate an empty path to /.

```python
from botocore.auth import SigV4Auth
from botocore.awsrequest import AWSRequest

import httpx

class AWSv4Auth(httpx.Auth):
    def __init__(self, aws_session, region, service):
        self.aws_session = aws_session
        self.region = region
        self.service = service

    def sign(self, request):
        aws_request = AWSRequest(
            method=request.method.upper(),
            url=to_canonical_url(request.url),
            data=request.body,
        )
        credentials = aws_session.get_credentials()
        SigV4Auth(credentials, service, region).add_auth(request)
        request.headers.update(**aws_request.headers.items())
        yield request
```

Let's create a class that uses botocore, the AWS Python SDK, to sign a request. You do that by faking an AWSRequest object with the canonical URL and the same data, asking for a signature, and grabbing the headers from the faked request.

Use this as follows.

```
client = httpx.Client(
    auth=AWSv4Auth(
        aws_session=botocore.session.get_session(),
        region='us-east-1',
        service='es',
    ),
)
```

In this case, the region and the service are part of the auth object. A more sophisticated approach would be to infer the region and service from the request URL and use that, which is beyond the scope of this example.

This should give a good idea about how custom authentication schemes work; write code that modifies the request to have the right authentication headers and then pass it as the auth parameter in the client.

7.5 Async client

HTTP calls can sometimes be slow. This might be because of network latency or server latency. Regardless, this means that doing several calls might take a long time.

As a stark example, httpbin.org has an endpoint, /delay, which waits a certain number of seconds. In this example, the code accesses it twice for different parameters.

```
import httpx, datetime

sync_client = httpx.Client()
before = datetime.datetime.now()
r1 = sync_client.get("https://httpbin.org/delay/3?param=sync-first")
r2 = sync_client.get("https://httpbin.org/delay/3?param=sync-second")
delta = datetime.datetime.now() - before
print(delta // datetime.timedelta(seconds=1))
results1 = r1.json()
```

```
results2 = r2.json()
print(results1["args"]["param"], results2["args"]["param"])
```

The processing, in this case, returns the parameter. In a real web API, the results would be more interesting. In this case, the interesting part is the time.

```
6
sync-first sync-second
```

This took six seconds since each call took three seconds.

One way to improve this is to use *asynchronous* network calls. The topic of asynchronicity in Python, in general, is beyond the scope of this chapter. It is important to mention that httpx supports async with a parallel API to the classic (synchronous) API.

```
import httpx, datetime
import asyncio

async def async_calls():
    before = datetime.datetime.now()
    async with httpx.AsyncClient() as async_client:
        fut1 = async_client.get("https://httpbin.org/
        delay/3?param=async-first")
        fut2 = async_client.get("https://httpbin.org/
        delay/3?param=async-second")
        responses = await asyncio.gather(fut1, fut2)
        delta = datetime.datetime.now() - before
    r1, r2 = responses
    results1 = r1.json()
    results2 = r2.json()
    print(delta // datetime.timedelta(seconds=1))
    print(results1["args"]["param"], results2["args"]["param"])

asyncio.run(async_calls())
```

The results are equivalent but faster.

```
3
async-first async-second
```

Note that just using await on each line would have still taken six seconds. To take advantage of async, the code separated launching the calls and waiting for the responses.

```
fut1 = async_client.get("https://httpbin.org/delay/3?param=async-first")
fut2 = async_client.get("https://httpbin.org/delay/3?param=async-second")
responses = await asyncio.gather(fut1, fut2)
```

Using await.gather() on both awaitable results allows both calls to start without delay.

7.6 Summary

Saying HTTP is popular feels like an understatement. It is everywhere—from user-accessible services through web-facing APIs and even internally in many microservice architectures.

httpx helps with all of these. It can be part of monitoring a user-accessible service for health, it can access APIs in programs to analyze the data, and it can be used to debug internal services to understand their state.

It is a powerful library with many ways to fine-tune it to send the right requests and get the right functions.

CHAPTER 8

Cryptography

Cryptography is a necessary component in many parts of a secure architecture. However, just adding cryptography to the code does not make it more secure; care must be given to such topics as secrets generation, secret storage, and plain-text management. Properly designing secure software is complicated, especially when cryptography is involved.

Designing for security is beyond the scope here. This chapter only teaches Python's basic tools for cryptography and how to use them.

8.1 Fernet

The cryptography module supports the Fernet cryptography standard. It is named after an Italian, not French, wine; the *t* is pronounced. A good approximation for the pronunciation is *fair-net*.

Fernet works for *symmetric* cryptography. It does not support partial or streaming decryption. It expects to read in the whole ciphertext and return the whole plain text. This makes it suitable for names, text documents, or even pictures. However, videos and disk images are a poor fit for Fernet.

The cryptographic parameters were Fernet, which were chosen by domain experts who researched available encryption methods and the known best attacks against them. One advantage of using Fernet is that it avoids the need to become an expert yourself. However, for completeness, note that the Fernet standard uses AES-128 in CBC padding with PKCS7, and HMAC uses SHA256 for authentication.

The Fernet standard is also supported by Go, Ruby, and Erlang and so is sometimes suitable for data exchange with other languages. It was specially designed, so using it *insecurely* is harder than using it correctly.

```
>>> k = fernet.Fernet.generate_key()
>>>  type(k)
<class 'bytes'>
```

© Moshe Zadka 2022
M. Zadka, *DevOps in Python*, https://doi.org/10.1007/978-1-4842-7996-0_8

The key is a short string of bytes. Securely managing the key is important; cryptography is only as good as its keys. If it is kept in a file, for example, the file should have minimal permissions and ideally be hosted on an encrypted file system.

The generate_key class method takes care to generate the key securely, using an operating system–level source of random bytes. However, it is still vulnerable to operating system–level flaws; for example, when cloning virtual machines, care must be taken that when starting the clone, it refreshes the source of randomness. This is admittedly an esoteric case, and whatever virtualization system is being used should have documentation on how to refresh the randomness source in its virtual machines.

```
>>> frn = fernet.Fernet(k)
```

The fernet class is initialized with a key. It makes sure that the key is valid.

```
>>> encrypted = frn.encrypt(b"x  marks  the  spot")
>>> encrypted[:10]
b'gAAAAABb1'
```

Encryption is simple. It takes a string of bytes and returns an encrypted string. Note that the encrypted string is *longer* than the source string. It is also signed with the secret key, which means that tampering with the encrypted string is detectable, and the Fernet API handles that by refusing to decrypt the string. The value gotten back from decryption is *trustworthy*. It was indeed encrypted by someone who had access to the secret key.

code:

```
>>> frn.decrypt(encrypted)
b'x marks the spot'
```

Decryption is done in the same way as encryption. Fernet does contain a version marker, so if vulnerabilities in these are found, it is possible to move the standard to a different encryption and hashing system.

Fernet encryption always adds the current date to the signed, encrypted information. Because of this, it is possible to limit the *age* of a message before decrypting.

```
>>> frn.decrypt(encrypted, ttl=5)
```

This fails if the encrypted information (sometimes referred to as the *token*) is older than five seconds. This is useful to prevent replay attacks, one where a previously encrypted token was captured and replayed instead of a new valid token. For example, if the encrypted token has a list of usernames that are allowed some access, and is retrieved using a subvertible medium, a user who is no longer allowed in can substitute the older token.

Ensuring token freshness would mean that no such list would be decoded, and everybody would be denied, which is no worse than if the medium was tampered with *without* having a previously valid token.

This can also be used to ensure good secret rotation hygiene. By refusing to decrypt anything older than, say, a week, you make sure that if the secret rotation infrastructure broke, you would fail loudly instead of succeeding silently and thus fix it.

The Fernet module also has a `MultiFernet` class to support seamless key rotation. `MultiFernet` takes a list of secrets. It encrypts with the first secret, but try decrypting with any secret.

If you add a new key to the end, it is first not used for encryption. After synchronizing the addition to the end, you can remove the first key. Now all encryptions are done via the second key, and even those instances where it is not synchronized yet have the decryption key available.

This two-step process is designed to have zero invalid decryption errors while still allowing key rotation, which is important as a precautionary measure. A well-tested rotation procedure means that if keys are leaked, the rotation procedure can minimize the harm they do.

8.2 PyNaCl

PyNaCl is a library wrapping the libsodium C library, which is a fork of Daniel J. Bernstein's libnacl. This is why PyNaCl is named the way it is. (NaCl, or sodium chloride, is the chemical formula for salt. The fork took the name of the first element.)

PyNaCl supports both symmetric and asymmetric encryption. However, since cryptography supports symmetric encryption with Fernet, the main use of PyNaCl is for asymmetric encryption.

The idea of asymmetric encryption is that there is a private and a public key. The public key can easily be calculated from the private key, but not vice versa; that is the asymmetry it refers to. The public key is published, while the private key must remain a secret.

There are, in general, two basic operations supported with public-key cryptography. You can encrypt with the public key in a way that can only be decrypted with the private key. You can also *sign* with the private key in a way that can be verified with the public key.

As discussed earlier, modern cryptographic practice places as much value on *authentication* as it does on *secrecy*. This is because if the media the secret is transmitted on is vulnerable to eavesdropping, it is often vulnerable to modification. Secret modification attacks have had enough impact on the field that a cryptographic system is not considered complete if it does not guarantee both authenticity and secrecy.

Because of that, libsodium, and by extension PyNaCl, do not support encryption without signing or decryption without signature verification.

To generate a private key, you just use the class method.

```
>>> from nacl.public import PrivateKey
>>> k = PrivateKey.generate()
```

The type of k is PrivateKey. However, at some point, you usually want to persist with the private key.

```
>>> type(k.encode())
<class 'bytes'>
```

The encode method encodes the secret key as a stream of bytes.

```
>>> kk = PrivateKey(k.encode())
>>> kk == k
True
```

You can generate a private key from the byte stream, and it is identical. This means you can again keep the private key in a way you decide is secure enough; a secret manager, for example.

In order to encrypt, you need a *public key*. Public keys can be generated from private keys.

```
>>> from nacl.public import PublicKey
```

```
>>> target = PrivateKey.generate()
>>> public_key = target.public_key
```

Of course, in a more realistic scenario, public keys need to be stored somewhere—in a file, in a database, or just sent via the network. For that, you need to convert the public key into bytes.

```
>>> encoded = public_key.encode()
>>> encoded[:4]
b'\xb91>\x95'
```

When you get the bytes, you can regenerate the public key. It is identical to the original public key.

```
>>> public_key_2 = PublicKey(encoded)
>>> public_key_2 == public_key
True
```

These bytes can be written to a file.

```
>>> with open("target.pubkey", "wb") as fpout:
...     fpout.write(encoded)
```

The PyNaCl Box class represents pair of keys; the first private, the second public. Box signs with the private key, then encrypts with the public key. Every message that you encrypt always gets signed.

```
>>> from nacl.public import PrivateKey, PublicKey, Box
>>> source = PrivateKey.generate()
>>> with open("target.pubkey", "rb") as fpin:
...     target_public_key = PublicKey(fpin.read())
>>> enc_box = Box(source, target_public_key)
>>> result = enc_box.encrypt(b"x marks the spot")
>>> result[:4]
b'\xe2\x1c0\xa4'
```

This signs with the source private key and encrypts using the target public key.

When you decrypt, you need to build the inverse box. This happens on a different computer, one that has the target *private key* but only the source *public key*.

127

```
>>> from nacl.public import PrivateKey, PublicKey, Box
>>> with open("source.pubkey", "rb") as fpin:
...     source_public_key = PublicKey(fpin.read())
>>> with open("target.private_key", "rb") as fpin:
...     target = PrivateKey(fpin.read())
>>> dec_box = Box(target, source_public_key)
>>> dec_box.decrypt(result)
b'x marks the spot'
```

The decryption box decrypts with the target private key and verifies the signature using the source public key. If the information has been tampered with, the decryption operation automatically fails. This means that it is impossible to access plain-text information that is not correctly signed.

Another piece of functionality that is useful inside of PyNaCl is cryptographic signing. It is sometimes useful to sign *without* encryption; for example, you can make sure to only use approved binary files by signing them. This allows the permissions for *storing* the binary file to be loose if you trust that the permissions on *keeping the signing key secure* are strong enough.

Signing also involves asymmetric cryptography. The private key is used to sign, and the public key is used to verify the signatures. This means that you can, for example, check the public key into source control and avoid needing any further configuration of the verification part.

You first must generate the private signing key. This is similar to generating a key for decryption.

```
>>> from nacl.signing import SigningKey
>>> key = SigningKey.generate()
```

You usually need to store this key (securely) somewhere for repeated use. Again, it is worthwhile remembering that anyone who can access the signing key can sign whatever data they want. For this, you can use encoding.

```
>>> encoded = key.encode()
>>> type(encoded)
<class 'bytes'>
```

The key can be reconstructed from the encoded version. That produces an identical key.

```
>>> key_2 = SigningKey(encoded)
>>> key_2 == key
True
```

For verification, you need to have the verification key. Since this is asymmetric cryptography, the verification key can be calculated from the signing key, but not vice versa.

```
>>>  verify_key  =  key.verify_key
```

You usually need to store the verification key somewhere, so you need to be able to encode it as bytes.

```
>>> verify_encoded = verify_key.encode()
>>> verify_encoded[:4]
b'\x08\xb1\x9e\xf4'
```

You can reconstruct the verification key. That gives an identical key. Like all ...Key classes, it supports a constructor that accepts an encoded key and returns a key object.

```
>>> from nacl.signing import VerifyKey
>>> verify_key_2 = VerifyKey(verify_encoded)
>>> verify_key == verify_key_2
True
```

When you sign a message, you get an interesting object back.

```
>>> message = b"The number you shall count is three"
>>> result = key.sign(message)
>>> result
b'\x1a\xd38[....'
```

It displays as bytes but are not bytes.

```
>>> type(result)
<class 'nacl.signing.SignedMessage'>
```

You can extract the message and the signature from it separately.

```
>>> result.message
b'The number you shall count is three'
>>> result.signature
b'\x1a\xd38[...'
```

This is useful if you want to save the signature in a separate place. For example, if the original is in object storage, mutating it might be undesirable. In those cases, you can keep the signatures on the side. Another reason is to maintain different signatures for different purposes or allow key rotation.

If you want to write the whole signed message, it is best to explicitly convert the result to bytes.

```
>>> encoded = bytes(result)
```

The verification returns the verified message, which is the best way to use signatures. This way, it is impossible for the code to handle an unverified message.

```
>>> verify_key.verify(encoded)
b'The number you shall count is three'
```

However, if it is necessary to read the object from somewhere else and then pass it into the verifier, which is also easy.

```
>>> verify_key.verify(b'The number you shall count is three',
...                   result.signature)
b'The number you shall count is three'
```

Finally, you can just use the result object as is to verify.

```
>>> verify_key.verify(result)
b'The number you shall count is three'
```

8.3 Passlib

Secure storage of passwords is a delicate matter. It is so subtle that it must deal with people who do not use password best practices. If all passwords were strong and people never reused passwords from site to site, password storage would be straightforward.

However, people usually choose passwords with little entropy (*123456* is still unreasonably popular, as well as *password*), they have a standard password that they use for all websites. They are often vulnerable to phishing attacks and social engineering attacks where they divulge the password to an unauthorized third party.

Not all threats can be stopped by correctly storing passwords, but many can. At the very least, they can be mitigated.

The Passlib library is written by people who are well versed in software security. It tries to eliminate the most obvious mistakes when saving passwords. Passwords are never saved in plain text; they are always hashed.

Note that hashing algorithms for passwords are optimized for different use cases than hashing algorithms used for other reasons; for example, one of the things they try to deny is brute-force source mapping attacks.

Passlib hashes passwords with the latest vetted algorithms optimized for password storage and intended to avoid any possibility of side-channel attacks. In addition, Salt is always used for hashing the passwords.

Although Passlib can be used without understanding these things, it is worthwhile to understand them to avoid mistakes while using Passlib.

Hashing means taking the users' passwords and running them through a reasonably easy function to compute but hard to invert. This means that even if an attacker gets access to the password database, they cannot recover users' passwords and pretend to be them.

One way that the attacker can attempt to get the original passwords is to try all combinations of passwords they can come up with, hash them, and see if they are equal to a password. To avoid this, special algorithms are used that are computationally hard. This means that an attacker would have to use a lot of resources to try many passwords so that even if, say, only a few million passwords are tried, it would take a long time to compare. Finally, attackers can use *rainbow tables* to pre-compute many hashes of common passwords and compare them all at once against a password database. To avoid that, passwords are salted before they are hashed; a random prefix (the salt) is added, the password is hashed, and the salt is prefixed to the hash value. When the user enters a password, the salt is retrieved from the beginning of the hash value before hashing it to compare.

Doing all of this from scratch is hard and even harder to get it right. Getting it right does not just mean having users log in but being resilient to the password database being stolen. Since there is no feedback about that aspect, it is best to use a well-tested library.

The library is storage agnostic. It does not care where the passwords are being stored. However, it does care that it is possible to update the hashed passwords. This way, hashed passwords can get updated to newer hashing schemes as the need arises. While Passlib does support various low-level interfaces, it is best to use the high-level interface of the CryptContext. The name is misleading since it does no encryption. It refers to vaguely similar (and largely deprecated) functionality built into Unix.

The first thing to do is decide on a list of supported hashes. Not all of them have to be *good* hashes; if you have supported bad hashes in the past, they still have to be on the list. In this example, you choose argon2 as the preferred hash but allow a few more options.

Using the argon2 hash, an extra dependency needs to be installed. Use pip install argon2_cffi to install it.

After installing argon2_cffi, construct a context for hashing passwords based on the guidelines discussed earlier.

```
>>> hashes = ["argon2", "pbkdf2_sha256", "md5_crypt", "des_crypt"]
```

Note that md5 and des have serious vulnerabilities and are not suitable for real application. You added them because there might be old hashes using them. In contrast, even though pbkdf2_sha256 is probably worse than argon2, there is no urgent need to update it. You want to mark md5 and des as deprecated.

```
>>> deprecated = ["md5_crypt", "des_crypt"]
```

Finally, after having made the decisions, you build the crypto context.

```
>>> from passlib.context import CryptContext
>>> ctx = CryptContext(schemes=hashes, deprecated=deprecated)
```

It is possible to configure other details, such as the number of rounds. This is almost always unnecessary, as the defaults should be good enough.

Sometimes you want to keep this information in some configuration (for example, an environment variable or a file) and load it; this way, you can update the list of hashes without modifying the code.

```
>>> serialized = ctx.to_string()
>>> new_ctx = CryptContext.from_string(serialized)
```

When saving the string, note that it does contain newlines; this might impact where it can be saved. If needed, it is always possible to convert it to base64.

When a user creates or changes a password, you need to hash the password before storing it. This is done via the hash method in the context.

```
>>> res = ctx.hash("good password")
```

When logging in, the first step is to retrieve the hash from storage. After retrieving the hash and having the users' passwords from the user interface, you need to check that they match and possibly update the hash if it is using a deprecated protocol.

```
>>> ctx.verify_and_update("good password", res)
(True, None)
```

If the second element were true, you would need to update the hash with the result. It is not a good idea to specify a specific hash algorithm but to trust the context defaults. However, you can force the context to hash with a weak algorithm to showcase the update.

```
>>> res = ctx.hash("good password", scheme="md5_crypt")
```

In that case, verify_and_update would let you know you should update the hash.

```
>>> ctx.verify_and_update("good password", res)
(True, '$5$...')
```

In that case, you would need to store the second element in the password hash storage.

8.4 TLS Certificates

Transport Layer Security (TLS) is a cryptographic way to protect data in transit. Since man-in-the-middle attacks are a potential threat, it is important to be able to verify that the endpoints are correct. For this reason, *certificate authorities* sign the public keys. Sometimes, it is useful to have a local certificate authority.

One case where that can be useful is in micro-service architectures, where verifying each service is the right one allows a more secure installation. Another useful case is for putting together an internal test environment, where using real certificate authorities is sometimes not worth the effort. It is easy enough to install the local certificate authority as locally trusted and sign the relevant certificates with it.

Another place this can be useful is in running tests. You want to set up a realistic integration environment when running integration tests. Ideally, some tests would check that TLS is used rather than plain text. This is impossible to test if you downgrade to plain-text communication for testing purposes. Indeed, the root cause of many production security breaches is that plain-text communication code inserted for testing was accidentally (or maliciously) enabled. Furthermore, it was impossible to test that such bugs did not exist because the testing environment *did* have plain-text communication.

For the same reason, allowing TLS connections without verification in the testing environment is dangerous. This means that the code has a non-verification flow, which can accidentally turn on, or maliciously be turned on in production and is impossible to prevent with testing.

Manually creating a certificate requires access to the hazmat layer in cryptography. This is so named because this is dangerous. You must judiciously choose encryption algorithms and parameters, and the wrong choices can lead to insecure modes.

To perform cryptography, you need a back end. This is because originally, it was intended to support multiple back ends. This design is mostly deprecated, but you still need to create it and pass it around.

```
>>> from cryptography.hazmat.backends import default_backend
```

Finally, you are ready to generate a private key. For this example, you use 2048 bits, which is considered reasonably secure as of 2018. A complete discussion of which sizes provide how much security is beyond the scope of this chapter.

```
>>> from cryptography.hazmat.primitives.asymmetric import rsa
>>> private_key = rsa.generate_private_key(
...     public_exponent=65537,
...     key_size=2048,
...     backend=default_backend()
... )
```

As always in asymmetric cryptography, it is possible (and fast) to calculate the public key from the private key.

```
>>> public_key = private_key.public_key()
```

This is important since the certificate only refers to the *public* key. Since the private key is never shared, it is not worthwhile and actively dangerous to make any assertions about it.

The next step is to create a *certificate builder*. The certificate builder adds assertions about the public key. In this case, you finish by *self-signing* the certificate since CA certificates are self-signed.

```
>>> from cryptography import x509
>>> builder = x509.CertificateBuilder()
```

You add names. Some names are required, though it is not important to have specific contents in them.

```
>>> from cryptography.x509.oid import NameOID
>>> builder = builder.subject_name(x509.Name([
... x509.NameAttribute(NameOID.COMMON_NAME, 'Simple Test CA'),
... ]))
>>> builder = builder.issuer_name(x509.Name([
... x509.NameAttribute(NameOID.COMMON_NAME, 'Simple Test CA'),
... ]))
```

You need to decide a validity range. For this, it is useful to have a day interval for easy calculation.

```
>>> import datetime
>>> one_day = datetime.timedelta(days=1)
```

You want to make the validity range start slightly before now. This way, it is valid for clocks with some amount of skew.

```
>>> today = datetime.datetime.now()
>>> yesterday = today - one_day
>>> builder = builder.not_valid_before(yesterday)
```

Since this certificate is for testing, you do not need to have it be valid for a long time. You make it valid for thirty days.

```
>>> next_month = today + (30 * one_day)
>>> builder  =  builder.not_valid_after(next_month)
```

The serial number needs to uniquely identify the certificate. Since remembering serial numbers is difficult, let's use random serial numbers. The probability of choosing the same serial numbers twice is extremely low.

```
>>> builder = builder.serial_number(x509.random_serial_number())
```

You then add the public key that you generated. This certificate is made of assertions *about* this public key.

```
>>> builder = builder.public_key(public_key)
```

Since this is a CA certificate, it needs to be marked as such.

```
>>> builder = builder.add_extension(
... x509.BasicConstraints(ca=True, path_length=None),
... critical=True)
```

Finally, after adding all the assertions to the builder, you need to generate the hash and sign it.

```
>>> from cryptography.hazmat.primitives import hashes
>>> certificate = builder.sign(
...     private_key=private_key, algorithm=hashes.SHA256(),
...     backend=default_backend()
... )
```

That's it! You now have a private key and a self-signed certificate that claims to be a CA. However, you need to store them in files.

The PEM file format is friendly to simple concatenation. Indeed, usually this is how certificates are stored; in the same file with the private key (since they are useless without it).

```
>>> from cryptography.hazmat.primitives import serialization
>>> private_bytes = private_key.private_bytes(
... encoding=serialization.Encoding.PEM,
... format=serialization.PrivateFormat.TraditionalOpenSSL,
... encryption_algorithm=serialization.NoEncrption())
```

```
>>> public_bytes = certificate.public_bytes(
... encoding=serialization.Encoding.PEM)
>>> with open("ca.pem", "wb") as fout:
...     fout.write(private_bytes + public_bytes)
>>> with open("ca.crt", "wb") as fout:
...     fout.write(public_bytes)
```

This gives you the capability to now be a CA.

For real certificate authorities, you generally need to generate a *certificate signing request* (CSR) to prove that the owner of the private key wants that certificate. However, since you are the certificate authority, you can just create the certificate directly.

There is no difference between creating a private key for a certificate authority and a private key for a service.

```
>>> service_private_key = rsa.generate_private_key(
...     public_exponent=65537,
...     key_size=2048,
...     backend=default_backend()
... )
```

Since you need to sign the *public key*, you must again calculate it from the private key.

```
>>> service_public_key = service_private_key.public_key()
```

You create a new builder for the service certificate.

```
>>> builder = x509.CertificateBuilder()
```

For services, the COMMON_NAME is important; this is what the clients verify the domain name against.

```
>>> builder = builder.subject_name(x509.Name([
... x509.NameAttribute(NameOID.COMMON_NAME, 'service.test.local')
... ]))
```

You assume that the service is accessed as service.test.local, using some local test resolution. Once again, you limit the certificate validity to about a month.

```
>>> builder = builder.not_valid_before(yesterday)
```

```
>>> builder = builder.not_valid_after(next_month)
```

This time, you sign the *service* public key.

```
>>> builder = builder.public_key(public_key)
```

However, you sign *with* the private key of the CA; you do not want *this* certificate to be self-signed.

```
>>> certificate = builder.sign(
...     private_key=private_key, algorithm=hashes.SHA256(),
...     backend=default_backend()
... )
```

Again, you write a PEM file with the key and the certificate.

```
>>> private_bytes = service_private_key.private_bytes(
... encoding=serialization.Encoding.PEM,
... format=serialization.PrivateFormat.TraditionalOpenSSL,
... encryption_algorithm=serialization.NoEncrption())
>>> public_bytes = certificate.public_bytes(
... encoding=serialization.Encoding.PEM)
>>> with open("service.pem", "wb") as fout:
...     fout.write(private_bytes + public_bytes)
```

The service.pem file is in a format that the most popular web servers can use: Apache, Nginx, HAProxy, and more. It can also be used directly by the Twisted web server through the txsni extension.

If you add the ca.crt file to the trusted root, and run, say, an Nginx server on an IP that the client would resolve from service.test.local, then when you connect clients to https://service.test.local, they verify that the certificate is valid.

8.5 Summary

Cryptography is a powerful tool, but one which is easy to misuse. Using well-understood high-level functions reduces many of the risks in using cryptography. While this does not substitute proper risk analysis and modeling, it does make this exercise somewhat easier.

Python has several third-party libraries with well-vetted code, and it is a good idea to use them.

CHAPTER 9

Paramiko

The Secure Shell Protocol (SSH) is commonly used to remotely manage Unix systems. SSH was originally invented as a secure alternative to the telnet command but soon became the de facto remote management tool.

Even systems that use custom agents to manage a server fleet, such as Salt, are often bootstrapped with SSH to install the custom agents. When a system is *described* as agent-less, as, for example, Ansible is, it usually means that it uses SSH as its underlying management protocol.

The Paramiko library implements an SSH client. This allows automating remote management of Unix systems using Python.

Paramiko has both high-level and low-level abstractions of the SSH protocol. This chapter covers, for the most part, the high-level abstractions.

Before delving into the details, it is worth noting the synergy Paramiko has with Jupyter. Using a Jupyter notebook, and running Paramiko inside it, provides a powerful auto-documented remote-control console. Having multiple browsers connected to the same notebook means it has a native ability to share troubleshooting sessions for remote servers without the need for cumbersome screen sharing.

The Paramiko library relies on a few *binary wheels* to implement the cryptographic operations that are part of the SSH protocol. On systems with good support for binary wheels, like Windows, macOS, or Linux distributions that use the GNU C Library, `pip install paramiko` installs the library without further work.

Installing Paramiko without using the binary wheels from PyPI for its dependencies can be more complicated. The official install guide covers the relevant steps and should be followed. These steps can, sometimes, change as dependencies are upgraded. For example, cryptography changed its tooling to take advantage of Rust, which means building it from a source requires a Rust compiler.

© Moshe Zadka 2022
M. Zadka, *DevOps in Python*, https://doi.org/10.1007/978-1-4842-7996-0_9

9.1 SSH Security

SSH allows you to *securely* control and configure remote hosts. However, security is a subtle topic. Even if the underlying cryptographic primitives, and the way the protocol uses them, are secure, you must use them properly to prevent misusage from causing an issue that opens the door for a successful attack.

It is important to understand how SSH thinks about security to use it securely. Unfortunately, it was built when affordance for security was not considered a high priority. It is easy to use SSH, which negates all security benefits gotten from it.

The SSH protocol establishes *mutual trust*. The client is assured that the server is authentic, and the server is assured that the client is authentic. There are several ways it can establish this trust, but this discussion covers the public key method. This is the most common one.

A server's public key is identified by a *fingerprint*. This fingerprint confirms the server's identity in one of two ways. One way is by being communicated by a previously established secure channel and saved in a file.

For example, when an AWS EC2 server boots up, it prints the fingerprint to its virtual console. The contents of the console can be retrieved using an AWS API call (which is secured using the Webs TLS model) and parsed to retrieve the fingerprint.

The other way is the Trust On First Use (TOFU) model. In the initial connection, the fingerprint is assumed to be authentic and stored locally in a secure location. On any subsequent attempts, the fingerprint is checked against the stored fingerprint, and a different fingerprint is marked as an error.

The fingerprint is a hash of the server's public key. If the fingerprints are the same, the public keys are the same. A server can prove that it knows the private key that corresponds to a given public key. In other words, a server can say here is my fingerprint and prove that it is indeed a server with that fingerprint. Therefore, if the fingerprint is confirmed

On the other side, users can indicate which public keys they trust to the server. Again this is often done via some out-of-band mechanism, a web API for the system administrator to put in a public key, a shared filesystem, or a boot script that reads information from the network. Regardless of how it is done, a user's directory can contain a file that means, "please authorize connections that can prove they have a private key corresponding to *this particular* public key as coming from me."

When an SSH connection is established, the client verifies the server's identity and then provides proof that it owns a private key corresponding to some public key on the server. If both steps succeed, the connection is verified in both directions and can be used for running commands and modifying files.

9.2 Client Keys

Client private and public keys are kept in files next to each other. Users often already have an existing key, but this is easily remedied if not.

Generating the key itself is easily done from Paramiko. I chose an Elliptic Curve Digital Signature Algorithm (ECDSA) key. Elliptic curve asymmetric cryptography has better resistance to attacks for the same key size than the older prime number–based cryptography. There is also much less progress in partial solutions to EC cryptography, so the consensus in the cryptographic community is that they are probably more secure against non-public actors.

```
>>> from paramiko import ecdsakey
>>> k = ecdsakey.ECDSAKey.generate()
```

As always with asymmetric cryptography, calculating the public part of the key from the private part is fast and straightforward.

```
>>> public_key = k.get_base64()
```

Since this is public, you do not have to worry about writing it to a file.

```
>>> with open ("key.pub", "w") as fp:
...     fp.write(public_key)
```

However, when you write out the private part of the key, you want to make sure that the file permissions are secure. You change the mode after opening the file but before writing any sensitive data to it.

Note that this is not perfectly safe. The file might have the wrong user if written to the wrong directory. Since some filesystems sync the data and metadata separately, a crash at exactly the wrong time can lead to the data being in the file but a bad file mode attached. This is only the *minimum* you need to do to safely write a file.

```
>>> import os
```

```
>>> with open ("key.priv",  "w") as fp:
...      os.chmod( "key.priv", 0o600)
...      k.write_private_key(fp)
```

The file mode is set to 0o600 *before* writing the sensitive bits to avoid race conditions. File modes are usually written as octal numbers, which is octal 600. If you write the bits corresponding to this octal code, they are 110000000, which translates to rw-------.

```
>>> import stat
>>> oct (stat.S_IWRITE I stat.S_IREAD)
'0o600'
```

This gives read and write permissions to the owner, no permissions to non-owner group members, and no permissions for anyone else.

Now through some out-of-band mechanism, push the public key to the relevant server.

For example, depending on the cloud service, code such as the following, where set_user_data is implemented using the cloud API, works on any server which uses cloudinit.

```
set_user_data(machine_id,
f"""
ssh_authorized_keys:
   - ssh-ecdsa   {public_key }
""")
```

Another thing that is sometimes done is using a Docker container as a bastion. This means you expect users to SSH both into the container and from the container into the spécific machine they need to run commands on.

In this case, a simple COPY instruction at build time (or a docker cp at runtime, as appropriate) accomplishes the goal. Note that it is perfectly fine to publish an image with public keys to a Docker registry. The requirement that this is a safe operation is part of the definition of public keys.

9.3 Host Identity

The TOFU principle is the most common first line of defense against man-in-the-middle attacks in SSH. After connecting to a host, its fingerprint must be saved in a cache for this to work.

The location of that cache used to be straightforward—a file in the user's home directory. However, more modern setups of immutable, throw-away environments, multiple user machines, and other issues complicate this.

It is hard to make a recommendation more general than share with as many trusted sources as possible. However, to enable that guideline, Paramiko does offer some facilities.

- A client can set a `MissingHostKeyPolicy`, which is an instance that supports an interface. This means that you can have logic to document the key or query an external database for it.

- The `known_hosts` file is an abstraction of the most common format on Unix systems, the `known_hosts` file. Paramiko shares the experience with keys with the regular SSH client by reading it and documenting new entries.

9.4 Connecting

While there are lower-level ways of connecting, the recommended high-level interface is SSHClient. Since their instances need to be closed, it is a good idea to use `contextlib.closing` as a context manager, if possible.

```
import contextlib, paramiko, sys

with contextlib.context(paramiko.SSHClient()) as client:
    client.connect(sys.argv[ 1])
    ## Do things witb client
```

When this is done at the top-level or as close to it as is reasonable, functions can accept `client` as an argument without worrying about lifetime. The connection is closed at the end of the stanza.

Sometimes, before connecting, various policies need to be configured on the client. This is sometimes useful in a function that returns a ready-to-connect client.

Some of the useful methods in preparing to connect are related to verifying authenticity; for example, set_missing_host_policy(policy).

import paramiko
```
client.set_missing_host_key_policy(paramiko.WarningPolicy())
```

In this case, the policy is set to WarningPolicy(). This policy uses the Python warnings module to warn about missing keys and allows the connection.

Policies are instances that define a method: policy. missing_host_key(client, name, key). The method should raise an error to prevent the connection. Any successful return is treated as a success.

To avoid missing the host, it is possible to load host keys into a client. Two methods can be used for that.

- load_system _host_keys() loads a file with host keys that should *not* be modified.

- load_host_keys () loads a file with host keys that should *not* be modified.

Other than whether the file is modified, the two methods have the same semantics and expect the same parameter.

from paramiko import SSHClient
import os

```
client.load_host_keys(os.path.expanduser( "-/.ssh/known_hosts" ))
```

This loads the known host's file, which is checked and updated by the command-line SSH tool. In this case, keys are automatically updated if the policy paramiko. AutoAddPolicy() is set as the policy.

Keys can also be explicitly saved.

```
client.save_host_keys(os.path.expanduser( "-/.ssh/known_hosts" ))
```

Note that only keys loaded via load_host_keys() are resaved. Keys loaded via load._system_host_keys() are not saved and are expected to be loaded again when recreating a client.

The connect method takes quite a few arguments. All of them except the hostname are optional. The following are the more important ones.

- hostname is the server to connect to.

- port is needed if you run on a special port other than 22. This is sometimes done as part of a security protocol; attempting a connection to port 22 automatically denies all further connections from the IP, while the real server runs on 5022 or a port that is only discoverable via API.

- username is the name of the user. While the default is the local user, this is less frequently the case. Often cloud virtual machine images have a default system user.

- pkey is a private key to use for authentication. This is useful if you want some programmatic way to get the private key (for example, retrieving it from a secret manager).

- allow_agent is True by default, for good reasons. This is often a good option since Paramiko never loads the private key. Therefore, no matter what happens, the private key itself cannot be compromised by anything inside the Python process; for example, accidentally logging a __dict__ of an instance.

- look.for.keys is set to False and gives no other key options to force using an agent.

9.5 Running Commands

The original SSH was invented as a telnet substitute, and its main job is still to run commands on remote machines. Note that remote is taken metaphorically, not always literally. SSH is sometimes used to control virtual machines and sometimes even containers that might be running close by.

After a Paramiko client has connected, it can run commands on the remote host. This is done using the exec_command client method. Note that this method takes the command to be executed as a *string*, not a list. This means that extra care must be exercised when interpolating user values into the command to make sure that it does not give a user complete execution privileges.

To print a "hello world" using Paramiko, you can use the following.

```
# Connect client
```

```
stdin, stdout, stderr = client.exec_command( "echo hello world" )
print (stdout.read().decode( "ascii"))
```

The return value of exec_command() is the command's standard input, output, and error. This means that the responsibility of communicating carefully with the command to avoid deadlocks is firmly in the hands of the end-user. The best way to do so is to avoid commands which read from standard input. If at all possible, create a file on the remote machine first.

The client also has an invoke_shell method, which creates a remote shell and allows programmatic access to it. It returns a Channel object connected directly to the shell. The send method on the channel sends data to the shell, just as if a person was typing at the terminal.

Similarly, the recv method allows retrieving the output. Note that this can be tricky to get right, especially around timing. In general, using exec_command is much safer. Opening an explicit shell is rarely needed, except for running commands that need interaction. For example, remotely running visudo requires real shell-like access.

9.6 Remote Files

To start file management, call the client's open_sftp method, which returns an SFTPClient object. You use methods on this object for all the remote file manipulation.

Internally, this starts a new SSH channel on the same TCP connection. This means that even while transferring files back and forth, the connection can still be used to send commands to the remote host. SSH does not have a notion of the current directory. Though SFTPClient emulates it, it is better to avoid relying on it and instead use fully qualified paths for all file manipulation. This makes code easier to refactor, and it does not have subtle dependencies on the order of operations.

9.6.1 Metadata Management

Sometimes you do not want to change the data but merely filesystem attributes. The SFTPClient object allows you to do the normal manipulation you expect.

The chmod method corresponds to os.chmod and takes the same arguments. Since the second argument to chmod is an integer interpreted as a permission bitfield, it is best expressed in octal notation. Thus, the best way to set a file to the regular permissions (read/write by owner, read to the world) is

```
client.chmod( "/etc/some_config", 0o644)
```

Note that the 0644 notation, borrowed from C, does not work in Python 3 (and is deprecated in Python 2). The 0o644 notation is more explicit and Pythonic.

Unfortunately, nothing protects you from passing in nonsense like

```
client.clunod( "/etc/some_ config", 644)
```

(This would correspond to -w----r-- in a directory listing, which is not insecure but very confusing!)

The following are some more metadata manipulation methods.

- chown changes the owner

- listdir_iter retrieves file names and metadata.

- stat, lstat retrieves file metadata.

- posix_rename atomically changes a file's name. (Do not use rename because it has confusingly different semantics; it is there for backward compatibility.)

- mkdir, rmdir creates and removes directories.

- utime sets the accessed and modified times of a file.

9.6.2 Upload

There are two main ways to upload files to a remote host with Paramiko. One is to simply use put. The easiest way is to give it a local path and a remote path and copy the file. The function also accepts other parameters, mainly a callback to call with intermediate progress. However, it is better to upload differently if such sophistication is required.

The open method on SFTPClient returns an open file-like object. It is straightforward to write a loop that remotely copies block by block or line by line. In that case, the logic for progress could be embedded in the loop itself instead of having to supply a callback function and carefully maintain states between calls.

9.6.3 Download

Much like uploading, there are two ways to retrieve files from the remote host. One is via the get method, which gets the names of the remote and local files, and manages the copying.

The other is again by using the open method, this time in read mode instead of write, and copying block by block or line by line. Again, if a progress indicator is needed or feedback from the user is desired, that is the better approach.

9.7 Summary

Most Unix-based servers can be managed remotely using the SSH protocol. Paramiko is a powerful way to automate management tasks in Python while assuming the least about any server. It runs an SSH server that you have permission to log in to.

CHAPTER 10

SaltStack

Salt belongs to a class of configuration management systems intended to make administrating a large number of machines easier. It does so by applying the same rules to different machines, making sure that any differences in their configuration are intentional.

It is written in Python and, more importantly, extensible in Python. For example, wherever a YAML file is used, Salt allows a Python file that defines a dictionary.

Salt adopts an open source model for its core code. The code can be cloned from the Salt source code repository. There are two PyPI packages available for Salt.

- The `salt` package includes the client/server code. It depends on `pyzmq`, which, in turn, relies on the libzmq C library.

- The `salt-ssh` package only includes the local and SSH-based client. Because of that, it does not depend on the libzmq library. When only local/SSH support is needed, it is better to install `salt-ssh`.

Other than this distinction, the two packages are identical.

10.1 Salt Basics

The Salt (or sometimes SaltStack) system is a *system configuration management* framework. It is designed to bring operating systems into a specific configuration. It is based on the convergence loop concept. When running Salt, it does three things.

- Calculates the desired configuration

- Calculates how the system differs from the desired configuration

- Issues commands to bring the system to the desired configuration

149

© Moshe Zadka 2022
M. Zadka, *DevOps in Python*, https://doi.org/10.1007/978-1-4842-7996-0_10

Some extensions to Salt go beyond the operating system concept to configure some SaaS products into the desired configuration; for example, there is support for Amazon Web Services, PagerDuty, or some DNS services (those supported by libcloud).

Since, in a typical environment, not all operating systems need to be configured the same way, Salt allows detecting properties of systems and specifying which configurations apply to which systems. Salt uses them at runtime to decide the complete desired state and enforce it.

There are a few ways to use Salt.

- Locally: Run a local command that takes the desired steps.

- SSH: The server will `ssh` into clients and run commands that take the desired steps.

- Native protocol: Clients connect to the server and take whatever steps the server instructs them.

Using the `ssh` mode removes the need to install a dedicated client on the remote hosts since, in most configurations, an SSH server is already installed. However, Salts native protocol for managing remote hosts has several advantages.

It allows the clients to connect to the server, thus simplifying discovery. All you need for discovery is just for clients to the server. It also scales better. Finally, it allows you to control which Python modules are installed in the remote client, which is sometimes essential for Salt extensions.

If some Salt configuration requires an extension that needs a custom module, you can take a hybrid approach. Use the SSH-based configuration to bring a host to the point where it knows where the server is and how to connect to it, and then specify how to bring that host to the desired configuration.

This means there are two parts to the server: one that uses SSH to bring up the system to a basic configuration which, among other things, has a Salt client, with the second part waiting for the client to connect to send the rest of the configuration.

This has the advantage of solving the secret bootstrapping problem. You verify the client hosts SSH key using a different mechanism, and when connecting to it via Salt, inject the Salt secret to allow the host to connect to it.

When you choose the hybrid approach, there needs to be a way to find all machines. When using some cloud infrastructure, it is possible to do this using API queries; however, you *need to make it accessible to Salt if you get this information.*

This is done using a *roster*. The roster is a YAML file. The top level is the logical machine name, which is important since this is how the machine is addressed using Salt.

```
file_server:                  # logical name of machine
    user: moshe               # username
    sudo: True                # boolean
    priv: /usr/local/key      # path to private key
print_server:                 # logical name of machine
    user: moshe               # username
    sudo: True                # boolean
    priv: /usr/local/key2 # path to private key
```

In ideal circumstances, all parameters are identical for the machines. The user is the SSH user. The sudo boolean states whether sudo is needed, which is almost always true. The only exception is if it is an administrative user (usually root). Since it is a best practice to avoid SSH as root, this is set to True in most environments.

The priv field is a path to the private key. Alternatively, it can be agent-forwarding to use SSH agent. This is often a good idea since it presents an extra barrier to key leakage.

The roster can go anywhere, but Salt looks for it in /etc/salt/roster by default. Putting this file in a different location is subtle. salt-ssh finds its configuration, by default, from /etc/salt/master. Since the usual reason to put the roster elsewhere is to avoid touching the /etc/salt directory, you usually need to configure an explicit master configuration file using the -c option.

Alternatively, a Saltfile can be used. salt-ssh looks to a Saltfile in the current directory for options.

```
salt-ssh:
  config_dir: some/directory
```

If you put in the value. In config_dir, it looks in the current directory for a master file. You can set the roster_file field in the master file to a local path (for example, roster) to make sure the entire configuration is local and locally accessible. This can help if a version control system is managing things.

After defining the roster, it is useful to check that the Salt system is functioning. It is also possible to run the commands to test Salt locally.

For testing locally, use `salt-call --local` instead of `salt '*'`. This needs privileged access, so it should probably be done in a VM or a container.

The following command sends a ping command to all the machines on the roster (or, later, all connected minions).

```
$ salt '*' test.ping
```

They are all supposed to return True. This command fails if machines are unreachable, SSH credentials are wrong, or other common configuration problems.

Because this command does not affect the remote machines, it is a good idea to run it first before starting to perform any changes. This ensures that the system is correctly configured.

Several other test functions are used for more sophisticated checks of the system.

The `test.false` command intentionally fails, which is useful to see what failures look like. For example, when running Salt via a higher-level abstraction, such as a continuous deployment system, this can be useful to see visible failures (for example, send appropriate notifications).

The `test.collatz` and `test.fib` functions perform heavy computations and return the time it took and a result. It is used to test performance; for example, this might be useful if machines dynamically tune CPU speed according to available power or external temperature. You want to test whether this is the cause of performance problems.

On the `salt` command line, many things are parsed into Python objects. The interaction of the shell parsing rules and the Salt parsing rules can sometimes be hard to predict. The `test.kwarg` command can be useful when checking how things are parsed. It returns the value the dictionary passed in as keyword arguments; for example, the following returns the dictionary of the keywords.

```
$ salt '*' test.kwarg word="hello" number=5 \
                    simple_dict='{thing: 1, other_thing: 2}'
```

The following shows the output when running locally with `salt-call --local test.kwarg`.

```
local:
    ----------
    __pub_fun:
        test.kwarg
    __pub_jid:
```

        20220221233400575283
    __pub_pid:
        858
    __pub_tgt:
        salt-call
    number:
        5
    simple_dict:
        ----
        other_thing:
            2
        thing:
            1
    word:
        hello

Since the combination of the shell parsing rules and the Salt parsing rules can be, at times, hard to predict, this is a useful command to be able to debug those combinations and figure out what things are over- or under-quoted.

Instead of `'*'` you can target a specific machine by logical name. This is often useful when seeing a problem with a specific machine. It allows a quick feedback mechanism when trying various fixes (for example, changing firewall settings or SSH private keys).

While testing that the connection works well is important, the reason to use Salt is to control machines remotely. While the main usage of Salt is to synchronize to a known state, Salt can also be used to run ad hoc commands.

```
$ salt '*' cmd.run 'mkdir /src'
```

This causes all connected machines to create a /src directory. More sophisticated commands are possible, and it is possible to only target specific machines.

The technical term for the desired state in Salt is *highstate*, which is shortened from *high-level state*. It describes the goal of the state. The name is a frequent cause of confusion because it seems to be the opposite of a low state, which is described almost nowhere.

The low states, or the low-*level* states, are the steps Salt takes to get to the goal. Since the compilation of the goal to the low-level states is done internally, nothing in the user-facing documentation talks about a low state, thus leading to confusion.

The following applies the desired state.

```
$ salt '*' state.highstate
```

Because a lot of confusion is caused by the name *highstate*, an alias was created.

```
$ salt '*' state.apply
```

Again, both do the same thing: figure out the desired state for all machines and then issue commands to reach it.

The state is described in SLS files. These files are usually in the YAML format and describe the desired state.

The usual way to configure is one file `top.sls,` which describes which other files apply to which machines. The `top.sls` name is used by default as the top-level file.

A simple homogenous environment might be as follows.

```
# top.sls
base:
  '*':
    - core
    - monitoring
    - kubelet
```

This example would have all machines apply the configuration from `core.sls` (presumably, making sure the basic packages are installed, the right users are configured, etc.), from `monitoring.sls` (presumably, making sure that tools that monitor the machine are installed and running), and `kubelet.sls`, defining how to install and configure the `kubelet`.

Indeed, much of the time, Salt configures machines for workload orchestration tools such as Kubernetes or Docker Swarm.

10.2 Salt Concepts

Salt introduces quite a bit of terminology and quite a few concepts.

A *minion* is the Salt agent. Even in the agentless SSH-based communication, there is still a minion. The first thing that Salt does is send over code for a minion and then start it.

A Salt *master* sends commands to minions.

A Salt *state* is a file with the `.sls` extension, which contains state declarations.

```
name_of_state:
  state.identifier:
    - parameters
    - to
    - state
```

For example:

```
process_tools:
  pkg.installed:
    - pkgs:
    - procps
```

This ensures the `procps` package (which includes the `ps` command among others) is installed.

Most Salt states are written to be *idempotent* to have no effect if they are already in effect. For example, if the package is already installed, Salt does nothing.

Salt *modules* are different from Python modules. Internally, they do correspond to modules, but only some modules.

Unlike *states*, modules *run* things. This means that there is no guarantee, or even attempt at, idempotence.

Often, a Salt state wraps a module with some logic to decide whether it needs to run the module; for example, before installing a package, `pkg.installed` checks if the package is already installed.

A *pillar* is a way of attaching parameters to specific minions, which different states can then reuse.

If a *pillar* filters out some minions, then these minions are *guaranteed* to never be exposed to the values in the pillar. This means that pillars are ideal for storing secrets since they are not sent to the wrong minions.

For better protection of secrets, it is possible to use `gpg` to encrypt secrets in pillars. Since `gpg` is based on asymmetric encryption, it is possible to advertise the public key; for example, in the same source control repository that holds the states and pillars.

This means anyone can add secrets to the configuration, but the private key is needed, on the master, to apply those configurations.

Since GPG is flexible, it is possible to target the encryption to several keys. As a best practice, it is best to load the keys into a gpg-agent. When the master needs the secrets, it uses gpg, which communicates with the gpg-agent.

This means the private keys are never exposed to the Salt master directly.

In general, Salt processes directives in states in order. However, a state can always specify require. When specifying dependencies, it is best to have the dependent state have a custom, readable name. This makes dependencies more readable.

```
Extract archive:
  archive.extracted:
    - name: /src/some-files
    - source: /src/some-files.tgz
    - archive_format: tar
  - require:
    - file: Copy archive
Copy archive:
  file.managed:
    - name: /src/some-files.tgz
    - source: salt://some-files.tgz
```

Having explicit readable names helps you make sure you depend on the right state. Note that even though Extract precedes Copy, it still waits for the copying to complete.

It is also possible to invert the relationship.

```
Extract archive:
  archive.extracted:
    - name: /src/some-files
    - source: /src/some-files.tgz
    - archive_format: tar
Copy archive:
  file.managed:
    - name: /src/some-files.tgz
    - source: salt://some-files.tgz
  - require_in:
    - archive: Extract archive.
```

In general, inverting the relationship does not improve things. However, this can sometimes be used to minimize or localize changes to files in a shared repository.

There are other relationships possible, and all of them can be inverted. `onchanges` specifies that the state should only be reapplied if another state has caused actual changes. `onfail` specifies that the state should only be reapplied if another state application fails. This can be useful to set alerts or make sure that the system goes back to a known state.

A few more esoteric relationships are possible, like `watch` and `prereq`, which are more specialized.

Minions generate keys when using the built-in Salt communication rather than the SSH method. Those keys need to be accepted or rejected. One way to do so is to use the `salt-key` command.

As mentioned, one way of bootstrapping the trust is to use SSH. Using Salt to transfer over parsed output from running `salt-key -F master` to the minion, and then set it in the minion's configuration under the `master_finger` field.

Similarly, run remotely `salt-call key.finger --local` on the minion (for example, with `salt 'minion' cmd. run`) and compare it to the pending key before accepting. This can be automated and leads to a verified chain.

There are other ways to bootstrap the trust, depending on what primitives are available. If, for example, hardware key management (HKM) devices are available, they can be used to sign the minions and the master's keys.

Trusted Platform Modules (TPM) can also mutually assure trust. Both mechanisms are beyond the current scope.

Grains (as in, a grain of salt) parameterize a system. They differ from pillars in that the *minion* decides on the grain, and that configuration is stored and modified on the minions.

Some grains, such as `fqdn`, are autodetected on the minions. It is also possible to define other grains in the minion configuration file.

It is possible to push grains from the master. It is also possible to grab grains from other sources when bootstrapping the minion. For example, it is possible to set the UserData as a grain on AWS.

Salt *environments* are directory hierarchies that each define a separate top file. Minions can be assigned to an environment, or an environment can be selected when applying the highstate using `salt '*' state.highstate saltenv=`....

`file_roots` is a list of directories that function like a path. When looking for a file, Salt searches `file_roots` in order. It can be configured on a per-environment basis and are the primary thing distinguishing environments.

10.3 Salt Formats

So far, the example SLS files were YAML files. However, Salt interprets YAML files as *Jinja templates* of YAML files. This is useful for customizing fields based on grains or pillars.

For example, the name of the package containing the things you need to build Python packages differs between CentOS and Debian.

The following SLS snippet shows how to target different packages to different machines in a heterogeneous environment.

```
{% if grains['os'] == 'CentOs' %}
python-devel:
{% elif grains['os'] == 'Debian' %}
python-dev:
{% endif %}
  pkg:
    - installed
```

It is important to notice that the Jinja processing step is completely ignorant of the YAML formatting. It treats the file as plain text, does the formatting, and then Salt uses the YAML parser on the result.

This means that Jinja can make an invalid file only in some cases. Indeed, you embedded such a bug in the preceding example. If the OS is neither CentOS nor Debian, the result would be an incorrectly indented YAML file, which fails to parse in strange ways.

To fix it, you want to raise an explicit exception.

```
{% if grains['os'] == 'CentOs' %}
python-devel:
{% elif grains['os'] == 'Debian' %}
python-dev:
{% else %}
{{ raise('Unrecognized operating system', grains['os']) }}
```

```
{% endif %}
  pkg:
    - installed
```

This raises an exception at the right point if a machine is added to the roster that is not one of the supported distributions. Otherwise, the YAML would be incorrectly formatted. In that case, the symptom would be that Salt would complain a parse error the YAML file, making it harder to troubleshoot the issue.

Such care is important whenever doing something non-trivial with Jinja because the two layers, the Jinja interpolation, and the YAML parsing, are not aware of each other: Jinja does not know it is supposed to produce YAML, and the YAML parser does not know what the Jinja source looked like.

Jinja supports *filtering* to process values. Some filters are built into Jinja, but Salt extends them with a custom list.

Among the interesting filters is YAML_ENCODE. Sometimes you need to have a *value* in the .sls file, which is YAML itself; for example, the content of a YAML configuration file that you need to be copied over.

Embedding YAML in YAML is often unpleasant; special care must be given to proper escaping. With YAML_ENCODE, it can encode values written in the native YAML.

For a similar reason, JSON_ENCODE_DICT and JSON_ENCODE_LIST are useful for systems that take JSON as input. The list of custom filters is long, and this is one of the frequent things that changes from release to release. The canonical documentation is on the Salt documentation site, docs.saltstack.com, under Jinja → Filters.

Until now, we referred to SLS files as files that are processed by Jinja and then YAML; however, this is inaccurate. It is the *default* processing, but it can override the processing with a special instruction.

Salt only cares that the final result is a YAML-like (or, equivalently in our case, JSON-like) data structure: a dictionary containing recursively dictionaries, lists, strings, and numbers.

Converting the text into such a data structure is called rendering in Salt parlance. This is opposed to common usage, where rendering means transforming *to* text and parsing means transforming *from* text, so it is important to note when reading Salt documentation.

A thing that can do rendering is a renderer. It is possible to write a custom renderer, but the most interesting is the py renderer among the built-in renderers.

Let's indicate that a file should be parsed with the py renderer with #!py at the top.

In that case, the file is interpreted as a Python file. Salt looks for a run function, runs it, and treats the return value as the state.

When running, __grains__ and __pillar__ contain the grain and pillar data.

As an example, you can implement the same logic with a py renderer.

```
#!py
def run():
    if __grains__['os'] == 'CentOS':
        package_name = 'python-devel'
    elif __grains__['os'] == 'Debian':
        package_name = 'python-dev'
    else:
        raise ValueError("Unrecognized operating system",
                         __grains__['os'])
return { package_name: dict(pkg='installed') }
```

Since the py renderer is not a combination of two unrelated parsers, mistakes are sometimes easier to diagnose.

You get the following if you reintroduce the bug from the first version.

```
#!py
def run():
    if __grains__['os'] == 'CentOS':
        package_name = 'python-devel'
    elif __grains__['os'] == 'Debian':
        package_name = 'python-dev'
return { package_name: dict(pkg='installed') }
```

In this case, the result is a NameError pinpointing the erroneous line and the missing name.

The trade-off is that reading it in YAML form is more straightforward if the configuration is big and mostly static.

10.4 Salt Extensions

Since Salt is written in Python, it is fully extensible in Python. The easiest way to extend Salt for new things is to put files in the `file_roots` directory on the Salt master. Unfortunately, there is no package manager for Salt extensions yet. Those files automatically get synchronized to the minions, either when running `state.apply` or explicitly running `saltutil.sync_state`. The latter is useful if you want to test, for example, a dry run of the state without causing any changes but *with* the modified modules.

10.4.1 States

State modules go under the root directory for the environment. If you want to share State modules between environments, it is possible to make a custom root and share that root between the right environments.

The following is an example of a module that ensures there are no files that have the name mean in them under a specific directory. It is probably not very useful, although making sure that unneeded files are not there could be important. For example, you might want to enforce no `.git` directories.

```
def enforce_no_mean_files(name):
    mean_files = __salt__['files.find'](name, path="*mean*")
    # ...continues below...
```

The name of the function maps to the name of the state in the SLS state file. If you put this code in `mean.py`, the appropriate way to address this state would be `mean.enforce_no_mean_files`.

The right way to find files or do anything in a Salt *state* extension is to call Salt executors. In most non-toy examples, this means writing a matching pair: a Salt executor extension and a Salt state extension.

Since you want to progress one thing at a time, you use a prewritten Salt executor: the `file` module, which has the `find` function.

```
def enforce_no_mean_files(name):
    # ...continued...
    if mean_files = []:
        return dict(
```

```
            name=name,
            result=True,
            comment='No mean files detected',
            changes=[],
        )
    # ...continues below...
```

One of the things the state module is responsible for, and often the most important thing, is *doing nothing* if the state is already achieved. This is what being a convergence loop is all about—optimizing to achieve convergence.

```
def enforce_no_mean_files(name):
    # ...continued...
    changes = dict(
        old=mean_files,
        new=[],
    )
    # ...continues below...
```

You now know what the changes are going to be. Calculating it here means you can guarantee consistency between the responses in the test vs. non-test mode.

```
def enforce_no_mean_files(name):
    # ...continued...
    changes = dict(
    if __opts__['test']:
        return dict(
            name=name,
            result=None,
            comment=f"The state of {name} will be changed",
            changes=changes,
        )
    # ...continues below...
```

The next important responsibility is to support the `test` mode. It is considered a best practice to always test before applying a state. You want to clearly articulate the changes that this module does if activated.

```
def enforce_no_mean_files(name):
    # ...continued...
    changes = dict(
    for fname in mean_files:
        __salt__['file.remove'](fname)
    # ...continues below...
```

In general, you should only be calling one function from the execution module that matches the state module. Since you are using file as the execution module in this example, you call the remove function in a loop.

```
def enforce_no_mean_files(name):
    # ...continued...
    changes = dict(
    return dict(
        name=name,
        changes=changes,
        result=True,
        comment=f"The state of {name} was changed",
    )
    # ...continues below...
```

Finally, you return a dictionary with the same changes as those documented in the test mode but with a comment indicating that these have already run.

This is the typical structure of a state module: one (or more) functions that accept a name (and possibly more arguments) and then return a result. The structure of checking if changes are needed and whether you are in test mode, and then performing the changes is also typical.

10.4.2 Execution

For historical reasons, execution modules go in the file roots _modules subdirectory. Similar to execution modules, they are also synchronized when state.highstate is applied and when explicitly synchronized via saltutil. sync_all.

As an example, let's write an execution module to delete several files to simplify the state module.

```
def multiremove(files):
    for fname in files:
        __salt__['file.remove'](fname)
```

Note that Salt is usable in execution modules as well. However, while it can cross-call other execution modules (in this example, `file`) it cannot cross-call into state modules.

You put this code in _modules/multifile, and you can change the state module to have

```
__salt__['multifile.mutiremove'](mean_files)
```

instead of

```
for fname in mean_files:
    __salt__['file.remove'](fname)
```

Execution modules are often simpler than state modules, as in this example. In this toy example, the execution module barely does anything except coordinate calls to other execution modules.

This is not completely atypical, however. Salt has so much logic for managing machines that all an execution module often has to do is coordinate calls to other execution modules.

10.4.3 Utility

When writing several execution or state modules, sometimes there is common code that can be factored out.

This code can sit in utility modules under the root file _utils directory. It is available as the __utils__ dictionary.

As an example, you can factor out the calculation of the return value in the state module.

```
def return_value(name, old_files):
    if len(old_files) == 0:
        comment = "No changes made"
        result = True
    elif __opts__['test']:
        comment = f"{name} will be changed"
```

```
        result = None
    else:
        comment = f"{name} has been changed"
        result = True
    changes = dict(old=old_files, new=[])
    return dict(
        name=name,
        comment=comment,
        result=result,
        changes=changes,
    )
```

You get a simpler state module if you use the execution module and the utility modules.

```
def enforce_no_mean_files(name):
    mean_files = __salt__['files.find'](name, path="*mean*")
    if len(mean_files) == 0 or __opts__['test']:
        return __utils__['removal.return_value'](name, mean_files)
    __salt__['multifile.mutiremove'](mean_files)
    return __utils__['removal.return_value'](name, mean_files)
```

In this case, you could have put the function as a regular function in the module. Putting it in a utility module was used to show how to call functions in utility modules.

10.4.4 Extra Third-Party Dependencies

Sometimes it is useful to have third-party dependencies, especially when writing new state and execution modules. This is straightforward to do when installing a minion. You just make sure to install the minion in a virtual environment with those third-party dependencies.

When using Salt with SSH, this is significantly less trivial. In that case, it is sometimes best to bootstrap from SSH to a real minion. One way to achieve that is to have a persistent state in the SSH minion directory and have the installation of the minion set a grain of completely_disable in the SSH minion. This would ensure that the SSH configuration does not cross-talk with the regular minion configuration.

10.5 Summary

Salt is a Python-based configuration management system. For non-trivial configurations, it is possible to *express* the desired system configuration using Python, which can sometimes be more efficient than templating YAML files. It is also possible to *extend* it with Python to define new primitives.

CHAPTER 11

Ansible

Like Puppet or Salt, Ansible is a configuration management system. Ansible does not have a custom agent. It usually works with SSH, though it also supports other modes, like Docker or local-based actions.

When using SSH, Ansible calculates the commands locally. It then sends simple commands and files through the SSH connection.

By default, Ansible tries to use the local SSH command as the control machine. If the local command is unsuitable, Ansible falls back to using the Paramiko library.

11.1 Ansible Basics

Ansible can be installed using `pip install ansible` in a virtual environment. After installing it, the simplest thing is to ping the localhost.

```
$ ansible localhost -m ping
```

This is useful since if this works, it means quite a few things are configured correctly: running the SSH command, configuring the SSH keys, and the SSH host keys.

The best way to use Ansible, as always when using SSH communication, is with a locally-encrypted private key that is loaded into an SSH agent. Since Ansible uses the local SSH command by default, if `ssh localhost` works the right way (without asking for a password), Ansible works correctly. If the localhost is not running an SSH daemon, replace the following examples with a separate Linux host, possibly running locally as a virtual machine.

Slightly more sophisticated, but still not requiring a complicated setup, is running a specific command.

```
$ ansible localhost -a "/bin/echo hello world"
```

© Moshe Zadka 2022
M. Zadka, *DevOps in Python*, https://doi.org/10.1007/978-1-4842-7996-0_11

You can also give an explicit address.

```
$ ansible 10.40.32.195 -m ping
```

Try to SSH to 10.40.42.195.

The set of hosts Ansible try to access by default is called the inventory. Specifying the inventory statically can be done using either an INI or a YAML format file. However, the more common option is to write an inventory script that generates the list of machines.

An inventory script is simply a Python file that can be run with the arguments --list and --host <hostname>. By default, Ansible uses the same Python to run the inventory script. It is possible to make the inventory script a real script running with any interpreter, such as a different version of Python, by adding a shebang line. Traditionally, the file is not named with .py. Among other things, this avoids accidental imports of the file.

When run with --list, it is supposed to output the inventory as formatted JSON. When run with --host, it is supposed to print the variables for the host. It is perfectly acceptable to always print an empty dictionary in these circumstances.

Here is a simple inventory script.

```python
#!/usr/bin/env python3
# save as simple.inv
import sys
import json

if '--host' in sys.argv[1:]:
    print(json.dumps({}))
else:
    print(json.dumps(dict(all='localhost')))
```

This inventory script is not very dynamic. It always prints the same thing. Run it with

```
$ chmod +x ./simple.inv
$ ./simple.inv
```

Though simple, it is a valid inventory script.
Use it with

```
$ ansible -i simple.inv all -m ping
```

This again pings (using SSH) the localhost.

Ansible is not primarily used to run ad hoc commands against hosts. It is designed to run playbooks. Playbooks are YAML files that describe tasks.

```
---
- hosts: all
  tasks:
    - name: hello printer
      shell: echo "hello world"
```

This playbook, which could be saved as echo.yml, runs echo "hello world" on all connected hosts.

The following runs it with the inventory script created.

```
$ ansible-playbook -i simple.inv echo.yml
```

This is the most common command to use when running Ansible day to day. Other commands are mostly used for debugging and troubleshooting, but the flow is to rerun the playbook a lot in normal circumstances.

By "a lot," I mean that playbooks should generally be written to be safely idempotent; executing the same playbook in the same circumstances again should not have any effect. In Ansible, idempotency is a property of the *playbook*, not of the basic building blocks.

For example, the following playbook is not idempotent.

```
---
- hosts: all
  tasks:
    - name: hello printer
      shell: echo "hello world" >> /etc/hello
```

One way to make it idempotent is to notice the file is already there.

```
---
- hosts: all
  tasks:
    - name: hello printer
      shell: echo "hello world" >> /etc/hello
      creates: /etc/hello
```

This notices the file exists and skips the command if so.

Instead of listing tasks in the playbooks, these are generally delegated to roles in more complex settings.

Roles are a way of separating concerns and flexibly combining them per host.

```
---
- hosts: all
  roles:
    - common
```

Then under `roles/common/tasks/main.yml`

```
---
- name: hello printer
  shell: echo "hello world" >> /etc/hello
  creates: /etc/hello
```

This does the same thing as earlier, but now it is directed through more files. The benefit is that if you have many different hosts and you need to combine instructions for some of them, this is a convenient platform to define parts of more complicated setups.

11.2 Ansible Concepts

When Ansible needs to use secrets, it has its internal vault. The vault has encrypted secrets and is decrypted with a password. Sometimes this password is in a file (ideally on an encrypted volume).

Ansible roles and playbooks are Jinja2 YAML files. This means they can use interpolation and support a few Jinja2 filters.

Some useful ones are `from/to_json/yaml`, which allows data to be parsed and serialized back and forth. The `map` filter is a meta-filter that applies an item-by-item filter to an iterable object.

Inside the filters, there is a set of variables defined. Variables can come from multiple sources: the vault (for secrets), directly in the playbook or role, or in files included from it. Variables can also come from the inventory (which can be useful if different inventories are used with the same playbook). The `ansible_facts` variable is a dictionary that has the facts about the current host: operating system, IP, and more.

They can also be defined directly on the command line. While this is dangerous, it can be useful for quick iterations.

In playbooks, it is often the case that you need to define both which user to log in as and which user (usually root) to execute tasks as.

Those can be configured on a playbook and overridden per task level.

The user that you log in as is `remote_user`. The user that executes is either `remote_user` if become is `False` or `become_user` if become is `True`. If become is `True`, the user switching is done by `become_method`.

The following are the defaults.

- `remote_user` – same as local user

- `become_user` – root

- `become` – False

- `become_method` – sudo

These defaults are usually correct, except for `become`, which often needs to be overridden to True. In general, it is best to configure machines so that, whatever you choose the `become_method` to be, the process of user switching does not require passwords.

For example, the following work on common cloud-provider versions of Ubuntu.

```
- hosts: databases
  remote_user: ubuntu
  become: True

  tasks:
  - name: ensure that postgresql is started
    service:
      name: postgresql
      state: started
```

If this is impossible, you need to give the argument `--ask-become-pass` to have Ansible ask for the credentials at runtime. Note that while this works, it hampers automation attempts, so it is best to avoid it.

Ansible supports patterns to indicate which hosts to update. In `ansible-playbook`, this is done with `--limit`. It is possible to do set arithmetic on groups: : means union, :! means set difference, and :& means intersection. In that case, the basic sets are the sets as defined in the inventory. For example, `databases:!mysql` limits the command to only `databases` hosts that are not MySQL.

Patterns can be regular expressions that match hostnames or IPs.

11.3 Ansible Extensions

You have seen one way to extend ansible using custom Python code: dynamic inventory. In the dynamic inventory example, you wrote an ad hoc script. The script, however, was run as a separate process. A better way to extend Ansible, and one that generalizes beyond inventory, is to use *plugins*.

An *inventory plugin* is a Python file. There are several places for this file so that ansible can find it. The easiest is `plugins/inventory_plugins` in the same directory as the playbook and roles.

This file should define a class called `InventoryModule` that inherits from `BaseInventoryPlugin`. The class should define two methods: `verify_file` and `parse`. The `verify_file` function is mostly an optimization. It is meant to quickly skip the parsing if the file is not the right one for the plugin. It is an optimization since `parse` can (and should) raise `AnsibleParserError` if the file cannot be parsed for any reason. Ansible then tries the other inventory plugins.

The `parse` function signature is

```
def parse(self, inventory, loader, path, cache=True):
    pass
```

The following is a simple example of parsing JSON.

```
def parse(self, inventory, loader, path, cache=True):
    super(InventoryModule, self).parse(inventory, loader, path, cache)
    try:
        with open(path) as fpin:
            data = json.loads(fpin.read())
    except ValueError as exc:
        raise AnsibleParseError(exc)
```

```
for host in data:
    self.inventory.add_host(server['name'])
```

The `inventory` object is how to manage the inventory. It has methods for `add_group`, `add_child`, and `set_variable`, which is how the inventory is extended.

The `loader` is a flexible loader that can guess a file's format and load it. The `path` is the path to the file which has the plugin parameters. Notice that if the plugin is specific enough, the parameters and the loader might not be needed in some cases.

The other common plugin to write is a lookup plugin. Lookup plugins can be called from the Jinja2 templates in Ansible to do arbitrary computation. This is often a good alternative when templates start getting too complicated. Jinja2 does not scale well to a complex algorithm or easily call into third-party libraries.

Lookup plugins are sometimes used for complex computation and sometimes for calling into a library to allow computing a parameter in a role. For example, it can take the name of an environment and calculate (based on local conventions) what are the related objects.

```
class LookupModule(LookupBase):

    def run(self, terms, variables=None, **kwargs):
        pass
```

For example, you can write a lookup plugin that calculates the largest common path of several paths.

```
class LookupModule(LookupBase):

    def run(self, terms, variables=None, **kwargs):
        return os.path.commonpath(terms)
```

Note that when *using* lookup modules, both `lookup` and `query` can be used from Jinja2. By default, `lookup` converts the return value into a string. The parameter `wantslist` can be sent to avoid a conversion if the return value is a list. Even in that case, it is important to only return a simple object—something composed only of integers, floats, and strings, or lists and dictionaries thereof. Custom classes are coerced into strings in various surprising ways.

11.4 Summary

Ansible is a simple configuration management tool that is easy to set up, requiring just SSH access. Writing new inventory and lookup plugins allows implementing custom processing with little overhead.

CHAPTER 12

Containers

Many modern applications are deployed as containers. Containers are a way of running applications in isolation. This isolation allows for building self-contained images with all dependencies an application needs to run.

There are several ways to run containers. A popular one used by Kubernetes and Docker is `containerd`.

For a container runner to run an application as a container, the application needs to be inside of an Open Container Initiative (OCI) image.

There are several ways to build images. The most popular ways—`buildctl, docker build`, and `nerdctl build`—wrap `buildkit`.

Internally, `buildkit` uses a format called Low-Level Builder (LLB), which is not designed for people to write container build specifications. Instead, many LLB front ends compile a specification.

The most common front end for LLB is `dockerfile.v0`. This front end is sometimes referred to as a `Dockerfile` because, by default, the front end looks for a file named `Dockerfile` as the source for the build specification.

The most common way to enable running Python code as a container is to write a `Dockerfile` containing a build specification. This `Dockerfile` is then given to `buildkit` to produce an OCI Image.

Writing a `Dockerfile` to build a Python application into a container image is different from writing a *good* `Dockerfile`. When creating container images, there are a lot of concerns to address.

Container images should be small, have fast build times, build reproducibly, and be easy to update with third-party security patches. These goals are, at least partially, in conflict with one another.

Making good choices or appropriate trade-offs when writing a `Dockerfile` for a Python application is why a good `Dockerfile` is subtle to achieve. It requires understanding the consequences of different ways of using the commands in a `Dockerfile` and how Python applications can be installed.

© Moshe Zadka 2022
M. Zadka, *DevOps in Python*, https://doi.org/10.1007/978-1-4842-7996-0_12

12.1 Choosing a Base Image

One of the first lines in a `dockerfile.v0` build specification starts with `FROM`. This indicates the base of the image. Images can be made from scratch, but starting from a popular Linux distribution is more common. Almost all distributions have an official container image or images.

12.1.1 GNU C Library Support

Because Python portable binary wheels (manylinux wheels) only support GNU C Library (glibc), it is usually good to stick to a glibc-based distribution. The most popular non-glibc-based distribution is Alpine Linux. It is possible to build Alpine-based container images for Python applications, but it is harder.

12.1.2 Long-Term Support

The packages installed in the container image, either in the base image or using the distributions package manager, inevitably have bugs or security issues. The container image needs to be rebuilt when there is a need to integrate a patch for a bug or security issue.

Such rebuilds can often be time-sensitive if the problem is urgent. Minimizing the changes needed to the container to integrate such fixes allows faster deployment. Less testing is required, and the chances that these changes require another part of the application to change are lower.

This makes rolling distributions, which integrate new upstream versions continuously, a bad fit as bases for Python-based container images. Distributions with conservative policy about adding changes to an existing release, and long-term security and bug fix support for a release, are better. Distributions like Arch and Fedora should be avoided as a base for Python-based container images.

12.1.3 Avoiding Unexpected Changes

Official distribution images hosted on public registries are regularly updated with fixes. This is true whether they are on general public registries such as `registy.hub.docker.com/library/debian` or ones with a more focused purpose like `registry.suse.com/suse/sle15`.

Even the images exposed under specific tags, such as `registry.suse.com/suse/sle15:15.3,` can change. In the case of SUSE, this can reflect `15.3.17.8.25` or `15.3.17.8.24`.

It is possible to address images by the specific digest, as shown in the following example.

```
FROM \
registry.hub.docker.com/library/debian@sha256:8a71adf557086b1f0379142a24cb
ea502d9bc864b890f48819992b009118c481
```

There is no guarantee that the digest is still available at the upstream registry. The old container image might get the garbage collector when a new image gets uploaded to the same tag.

A good practice is to keep the base image in a locally controlled registry. It should be updated regularly, but tags and versions are now under direct local control; for example, images can be tagged by the pulling date and guaranteed to last 60 days. The images, tags, frequency of pulling, and expiration policies should be clearly documented. It is often useful to centralize this process and support a small number of organization-wide blessed base images.

How centralized the process should be and how many base images to support depends on local needs, compliance requirements, and the size of the organization. This can be a contentious issue. One way to partially mitigate that is to clearly document the process and the trade-offs made and how decisions were made.

12.2 Installing the Python Interpreter

There are a few potential sources for the Python interpreter. Native Python distributions have a few downsides.

- A Python distribution is optimized for distributing Python packages; it is not optimized to be a development platform.

- New versions of Python, even patch versions, might not be available until a new version of the distribution is available.

12.2.1 conda

One option is installing conda and then installing Python in a conda environment. This is a good option if you are willing to commit to conda, creating conda environments, and installing things inside them.

This option is especially attractive when needing other features of conda, such as the availability of prebuilt binaries that are not Python-specific. This can be useful, especially in containers for data science and machine learning applications.

Unless the application developers are already using conda as their day-to-day development environment, adding another tool that developers must be familiar with can have significant downsides. This is not the best choice to get a Python interpreter in those cases.

12.2.2 Third-Party Repositories

Some third-party repositories, like deadsnakes for Ubuntu, build versions of Python designed to be used for development. Adding these repositories as an extra upstream, and installing Python through them, is one way to get Python into a container image.

Some due diligence should be done to vet the build process and options to make sure the Python builds are appropriate for the application. It is also important to understand how soon a new version of Python is available through the repository after it is released.

12.2.3 Building Python in the Container

The pyenv tool downloads and installs a version of Python. It can be used on any Unix-like operating system, including containers.

When pyenv builds and deploys Python, it also deploys shims. These are designed to switch between versions of Python.

Since a container image usually only has one version of Python, these shims are superfluous. It is possible to build Python directly with `python-build`, a pyenv subproject.

Finally, it is possible to download the source code from Python.org, unpack it, and run it.

Regardless of which one is used, this is time-consuming and requires quite a few build requirements. Because of this, this is usually done as an internal base image build, which is then used by an application-specific image build. Using a multistage build, where the Python interpreter's directory is copied to the second, can avoid the build dependencies.

The directory also contains some things which are not needed in a runtime image. For example, the tests and static libraries are not useful.

It is important to verify that some built-in modules are correctly built, or some packages fail in strange ways. Some of the usual culprits are `ssl`, `sqlite3`, and `lzma`.

12.2.4 Python Base Image

If Debian as a base is a reasonable choice, the `python` images on Docker Hub are a useful alternative. Note that images intended for runtime should be started from a `-slim` variant.

12.3 Installing Python Applications

A container image for a Python application has to have an application installed. It is almost always the base that a dedicated virtual environment, or a conda environment, is a good idea.

Although a container image only runs one application, having the application in a virtual environment costs little and simplifies a few potential next steps. The most important is that virtual environments can be copied from one stage to the next.

This allows the application to be installed in a stage that, for example, includes installing any relevant build tools for dependencies or other steps. The runtime stage does not need these tools, only the installed version in the virtual environment.

After creating the virtual environment and installing any non-Python dependencies, the next step is to install the Python dependencies. Dependencies should be installed from a `requirements.txt` file.

When using Poetry or Pipenv, it makes sense to export the `requirement.txt` file from those systems. Otherwise, `pip-compile` can be used for that.

In either case, `requirements.txt` should be *checked in* and not generated during the build process. This makes the container image build reproducible; rebuilding the image at a later date installs the same dependencies.

After installing the dependencies, the application itself needs to be installed. The best way to do it is in two steps.

- `python -m build` to generate a wheel

- Install the wheel using `pip install --no-dependencies`

Separating the build step from the install step means that the build does not need to be installed in the virtual environment for the runtime. Installing without dependencies means that no superfluous dependencies are installed.

After installing, use `pip check` in the environment to check that there are no missing dependencies and that all versions are compatible.

Since the results of `pip check` depend only on the wheel and the `requirements.txt` file, this depends only on the source code.

A container image build step can be added to the continuous integration system workflow that is triggered on suggested code patches (pull requests or merge requests). If such a step is added, it can be made into a "gating" step: code changes cannot be merged unless it succeeds. Installing versions of the dependencies that are described in the source code, and having the container build verified in continuous integration, allows for confidence when building the image on the main branch. Since container images built from the main branch are often the ones used in production, this is an important goal.

Putting it all together, a `Dockerfile` for an application that uses Pyramid might look like the following.

```
FROM python:bullseye as venv-builder

RUN pip install build
RUN mkdir /src/
WORKDIR /src
RUN python -m venv /opt/pyr-venv/
COPY requirements.txt /src/
RUN /opt/pyr-venv/bin/pip install -r /src/requirements.txt
COPY setup.cfg pyproject.toml /src/
# copy source code
RUN python -m build
RUN /opt/pyr-venv/bin/pip install --no-dependencies dist/*.whl
RUN /opt/pyr-venv/bin/pip check
```

```
FROM python:slim-bullseye as runtime
COPY --from=venv-builder /opt/pyr-venv /opt/pyr-venv
```

The setup.cfg file only declares loose dependencies.

```
[metadata]
name = pyrapp
version = 0.0.1

[options]
install_requires =
    pyramid
    gunicorn
```

The requirements.txt file has complete, pinned dependencies.

```
$ wc -l requirements.txt
33 requirements.txt
$ egrep 'pyramid|gunicorn' requirements.txt |grep -v '#'
gunicorn==20.1.0
pyramid==2.0
```

If a requirement is added to the setup.cfg, the build fails.

```
$ tail -4 setup.cfg
install_requires =
    pyramid
    gunicorn
    attrs
$ docker build .
...
Step 11/13 : RUN /opt/pyr-venv/bin/pip check
---> Running in 6a186bd1f533
pyrapp 0.0.1 requires attrs, which is not installed.
The command '/bin/sh -c /opt/pyr-venv/bin/pip check' ...
```

12.4 Optimizing Container Build Cache

The `buildkit` container image build has sophisticated caching capabilities. Understanding how to use those can improve build speed by a significant amount.

The first thing to consider is the base image. Neither the distribution packages nor the Python interpreter tends to change often. Even the most diligent of compliance policies do not require updating with security patches that have been released for less than a day.

In other words, creating a daily image with the latest distribution packages and the desired Python version can be done daily. The base can be tagged with the date.

For example, it can follow a naming convention like `internal-registry.example.com/base-python-image:3.9-2022-03-10`. An `ONBUILD` instruction can be used to enforce a compliance policy, such as refusing to build if the date is more than 60 days from the build date.

The advantage of enacting such a policy is that the first line in a `Dockerfile` can start with a specific `FROM` image.

```
FROM internal-registry.example.com/base-python-image:3.9-2022-03-10
```

Since this image never changes, the cache is not invalidated by a new image uploaded to this tag. When images change, cache behavior can be dependent on local configuration. It either invalidates the entire cache, or it might not notice it.

In the latter cache, the advice is sometimes to build without caching. This makes container image builds slower and more frustrating.

The first line is all-important because all other steps must be re-executed if it invalidates the cache. It is worth it to carefully tune it to improve container image build times.

After this line, the next step is to be careful about `COPY` lines and do as much work as possible before another `COPY` line.

Look at the following example.

```
COPY requirements.txt setup.cfg ... /app/sources/
RUN python -m venv /app/runtime/
RUN /app/runtime/bin/pip install -r /app/sources/requirements.txt
RUN pip install build
RUN cd /app/sources/ && python -m build
RUN /app/runtime/bin/pip install --no-dependencies /app/sources/dist/*.whl
```

Instead, it is better to move the pip install build line to the base build, removing the need to carefully manage the dependencies of build while still generating reproducible builds.

The remaining lines are better off broken and reordered.

```
RUN python -m venv /app/runtime/
```

Creating the virtual environment is a reasonably fast operation. However, there is no need to delay it. It does not depend on files and can be cached forever or if the FROM line is the same.

```
COPY requirements.txt /app/sources/
RUN /app/runtime/bin/pip install -r /app/sources/requirements.txt
```

Copying only the requirements.txt allows the cache to avoid rerunning the pip install if this file has not changed. Re-pinning the dependency list is not a frequent process; even the most diligent programmer rarely updates more than once per day.

```
COPY setup.cfg ... /app/sources/
RUN cd /app/sources/ && python -m build
RUN /app/runtime/bin/pip install --no-dependencies /app/sources/dist/*.whl
```

This part depends on every single source file, the most volatile part of the code. It is also pretty fast in general. The most time-consuming step is python -m build since it might require installing dependencies in a virtual environment.

If this might be a problem, there is a solution. The following runs a mock build, which might fail, with only pyproject.toml and setup.cfg copied.

```
COPY setup.cfg pyproject.toml /app/sources/
RUN cd /app/sources/ && (python -m build --no-isolation || true)
RUN rm -rf /app/soures/dist
COPY setup.cfg ... /app/sources/
RUN cd /app/sources/ && python -m build --no-isolation
RUN /app/runtime/bin/pip install --no-dependencies /app/sources/dist/*.whl
```

Adding --no-isolation installs the build dependencies in the environment where build is installed. The first run primes installing the build dependencies.

The pyproject.toml and setup.cfg files tend to change less than the Python source code itself. Because priming is invalidated only if one of those files changes, it allows caching the installation of the build dependencies.

The real `python -m build` run does not need to reinstall these dependencies. This means that changing only Python code and running another container image build does not require reinstalling the build dependencies.

Carefully considering which files change and how often and copying files at the right point can make a big difference in build times.

When using continuous integration to build images, it is a good idea to export and import the cache from a persistent store. Often CI (Continuous Integration) workers are short-lived. The correct persistent store to use depends on factors like availability and the CI system itself.

After optimizing the `Dockerfile` to take advantage of the cache, it is worthwhile to spend time considering how to use this cache correctly in CI. The `buildkit` documentation covers which caches are available and how to use them, including `registry`, `inline`, `local`, and a specialized one for GitHub actions: `gha`.

12.5 Rebuilding Containers

Building containers reproducibly and in a cache-friendly way means that the dependencies are not upgraded when running a new build. This is good for predictability, but dependencies should be eventually upgraded.

Since dependencies eventually need to be upgraded, it is easier to *continuously* upgrade them. Otherwise, the latest version might be far ahead of the current version when needing to upgrade.

Most open source projects try to deprecate things slowly and mindfully. Upgrading to a newer version might require changes, but rarely big changes. Upgrading to a version that is a year ahead might be much harder.

Some upgrades need to be done quickly, such as integrating a patch for a security fix. Upgrading continuously builds up the experience to make those upgrades much easier.

This means that regularly rebuilding on top of the newest dependencies is the best practice. A good frequency is between one to two weeks.

Do the following when upgrading.

1. Regenerate the `requirements.txt`, pinning to the latest versions.

2. Update the `FROM` header to use the latest date (or one day before).

Because both the `Dockerfile` and the `requirements.txt` file are under source control, this can be handled no differently than any other merge request. It can be generated automatically or semi-automatically.

Regardless of how it is generated, it needs to go through the usual development cycle. This usually means a green continuous integration result on the branch. It might also mean a manual or automated run against a staging environment. If either fails, and the branch cannot be merged, it should be the responsibility of someone in the team to triage and fix it.

If the immediate fix is too big, usually, this is the cause of one or two new dependencies. Those dependencies can be pinned in the source (for example, `setup.cfg` when using `setuptools`, or `Pipenevif` using Pipenv).

This should be treated as a temporary solution. A good practice is to annotate those pins linked to a ticket or issue in the ticket management system and prioritize those.

There are some tools to automate the creation of these change requests. Using them, at least, alleviates needing to remember to generate the requests. The other tasks, reviewing the CI, checking what other tests need to happen before the merge, and triaging problems, are usually harder to automate.

12.6 Container Security

There are three important things to keep in mind to improve the security of a container image.

- Avoid unneeded files

- Keep dependencies up to date

- Follow the principle of least privilege

A good technique to reduce unneeded files is to use a multistage build and copy over the virtual environment, as shown earlier. Keeping dependencies up to date is mostly an exercise updating regularly, as shown earlier.

The last part to cover is the principle of least privilege. To do that at all, the processes in the container should not be run as root. This can be done at container image build time by ensuring there is a less-privileged user, say `runtime`, and including a line to set the default user executing the processes.

```
USER runtime
```

Even without any other work, this already eliminates, or makes significantly harder, a few potential attacks. For example, most container-escape attacks depend on root privileges. Forcing an attacker to find a root escalation hole makes attacks harder, takes more time, and potentially triggers more auditing events, allowing a security team to respond.

Security can further be improved by giving the runtime user few file system access permissions. If it is possible to make no part of the file system writable by this user, this is best. If it is not possible to eliminate file system writes completely, the virtual environment running the process should not be writable by this user.

One way to test that is to `pip install` in a test that uses the resulting container image. If the `pip install` succeeds, the test should fail.

12.7 Summary

Python is a popular language for different kinds of back-end applications, such as machine learning and web applications. These applications are often built into container images and then deployed into various container runtimes.

Building a container image that hosts a Python application should balance the local considerations. Typical considerations include development speed, being able to ship hotfixes, and being able to update when new security fixes become available.

Rather than being reactive, gather the requirements in advance and build a container image build process that satisfies them. When different criteria need to be traded off against each other, it is easier to do such trade-offs in advance rather than as a response to an emergency.

When done well, container images can be a part of the developer experience throughout the software development life cycle. This eliminates a source of friction: differences between the developer environments and the production environment. Building good container images is not a complete solution for this, but it is a necessary part.

CHAPTER 13

Amazon Web Services

Amazon Web Services (AWS) is a popular cloud platform. It allows using computation and storage resources in a data center and other services.

Amazon provides a *free tier* for some services. In general, services are pay-by-usage.

Note When experimenting with AWS, note that you are charged for any services you consume. Monitor your billed usage carefully, and turn off any services you do not use to avoid paying more than you intend.

This chapter is not, and cannot be, a comprehensive introduction to all AWS services. It explains some specific ways to interact with some of the services using Python and some general techniques for using AWS API through **API.**

One of the central principles of AWS is that all interactions with it should be possible via an API. The web console, where computing resources can be manipulated, is just another front-end to the API. This allows automating the infrastructure configuration—infrastructure as code, where the computing infrastructure is reserved and manipulated programmatically.

The Amazon Web Services team supports a package on PyPI, boto3, to automate AWS operations. This is one of the best ways to interact with AWS.

Note There are different ways to configure boto3. Setting the AWS_DEFAULT_ REGION environment variable to an AWS region, such as us-west-2, means that passing an explicit region name to boto3 setup functions is optional. Some of the examples in this chapter take advantage of that to focus on other aspects of the library or AWS.

M. Zadka, *DevOps in Python*, https://doi.org/10.1007/978-1-4842-7996-0_13

While AWS does support a console UI, it is usually best to use that as a read-only window into AWS services. When making changes through the console UI, there is no repeatable record of it. While it is possible to log actions, this does not help reproduce them.

Combining `boto3` with Jupyter, as discussed in an early chapter, makes for a powerful AWS operations console. Actions taken through Jupyter, using the `boto3` API, can be repeated, automated, and parameterized as needed.

When making ad hoc changes to the AWS setup to solve a problem, it is possible to attach the notebook to the ticket tracking the problems to have a clear record of what was done to address the problem. This serves both to understand what was done if this caused some unforeseen issues and to easily repeat this intervention if this solution is needed again.

As always, notebooks are not an *auditing* solution; for one, when allowing access via `boto3`, actions do not have to be performed via a notebook. AWS has internal ways to generate *audit* logs. The notebooks are there to document intent and allow repeatability.

13.1 Security

For automated operations, AWS requires *access keys*. Access keys can be configured for the root account, but this is not a good idea. There are no restrictions possible on the root account, so this means that these access keys can do everything.

AWS platform for roles and permissions is called *identity and access management* (IAM). The IAM service is responsible for users, roles, and policies.

In general, it is better to have a separate IAM user for each human user and each automated task that needs to be taken. Even if they all share an access policy, having distinct users means it is easier to do key management and have accurate audit logs of who (or what) did what.

13.1.1 Configuring Access Keys

With the right security policy, users can be in charge of their own access keys. A single access key comprises the access key *ID* and the access key *secret*. The *ID* does not need to be kept secret and remains accessible via the IAM user interface after generation. This allows, for example, disabling or deleting an access key by ID.

A user can configure up to two access keys. Having two keys allows for doing 0-downtime key rotations. The first step is to generate a new key. Then replace the old key everywhere. Afterward, disable the old key. *Disabling* the old key makes anything that tries to use it fail. If such a failure is detected, it is easy to *re-enable* the old key until the task using that key can be upgraded to the new key.

After a certain amount of time, when no failures have been observed, it should be safe to delete the old key.

Local security policies generally determine how often keys should be rotated, but this should usually be at least a yearly ritual. This should generally follow practices for other API secrets used in the organization.

Note that in AWS, different computation tasks can have their own IAM credentials.

For example, an EC2 machine can be assigned an IAM role. Other higher-level computation tasks can also be assigned a role. For example, an Elastic Container Service (ECS) task, which runs one or more containers, can be assigned an IAM role. Serverless Lambda functions, which run on infrastructure allocated on an as-needed basis, can also be assigned an IAM role.

The boto3 client automatically uses these credentials if running from such a task. This removes the need to explicitly manage credentials and is often a safer alternative.

13.1.2 Creating Short-Term Tokens

AWS supports short-term tokens (STS), which can be used for several things. They can be used to convert alternative authentication methods into tokens that can be used with any boto3-based program, for example, by putting them in an environment variable.

For example, the following code takes the configured *default credentials* and uses them to get a short-term token for a role.

```
import boto3

response = client.assume_role(
    DurationSeconds=120,
    RoleArn='arn:aws:iam::123456789012:role/demo',
)
credentials = response['Credentials']
session = boto3.Session(
    aws_access_key_id=credentials['AccessKeyId'],
```

```
    aws_secret_access_key=credentials['SecretAccessKey'],
    aws_session_token=credentials['SessionToken'],
)
print(session.client('ec2').describe_instances())
```

This can be used to improve auditing or to reduce the security impact of lost or stolen credentials.

A more sophisticated example could be used in a web portal with assume_role_with_saml.

```
import boto3
import base64

def credentials_from_saml_assertion(assertion):
    assertion = base64.b64encode(assertion.encode("ascii")).decode("ascii")
    response = boto3.client('sts').assume_role_with_saml(
        RoleArn='arn:aws:iam::123456789012:role/demo',
        PrincipalArn='arn:aws:iam::123456789012:role/princpal',
        SAMLAssertion=assertion,
        DurationSeconds=120
    )
    return response['Credentials']
```

With this logic, the web portal has no special access to the AWS account. After the user logs in, it uses the assertion to create a short-term token for operations.

On an account that has been configured with cross-account access, assume_token can return credentials for the granting account.

Even when using a single account, sometimes it is useful to create a short-term token. For example, this can be used to limit permissions. It is possible to create an STS with a limited security policy. Using limiting tokens in code that is more prone to vulnerabilities, such as direct user interactions, limits the attack surface.

13.2 Elastic Computing Cloud (EC2)

The Elastic Computing Cloud (EC2) is the most basic way to access AWS compute (CPU and memory) resources. EC2 runs machines of various types. Most are virtual machines (VMs) that run with other VMs on physical hosts. The AWS infrastructure takes care of fairly dividing resources between the VMs.

The EC2 service also handles the resources that machines need to work properly: operating system images, attached storage, and networking configuration, among others.

13.2.1 Regions

EC2 machines run in regions. Regions usually have a human-friendly name (such as Oregon) and an identifier used for programs (such as us-west-2).

There are several regions in the United States, including North Virginia (us-east-1), Ohio (us-east-2), North California (us-west-1), and Oregon (us-west-2). There are also several regions in Europe, Asia Pacific, and more.

When you connect to AWS, you connect to the region you need to manipulate; `boto3.client("ec2", region_name="us-west-2")` returns a client that connects to the Oregon AWS data center.

It is possible to specify default regions in environment variables and configuration files, but it is often best to be explicit in code (or retrieve it from higher-level application configuration data).

EC2 machines also run in the *availability zone*. While regions are objective (every customer sees the region the same), availability zones are not: one customer's us-west-2a might be another's us-west-2c.

Amazon puts all EC2 machines into a virtual private cloud (VPC) network. For simple cases, an account has one VPC per region, and all EC2 machines belonging to that account are in that VPC.

A *subnet* is how a VPC intersects with an availability zone. All machines in a subnet belong to the same zone. A VPC can have one or more *security groups*. Security groups can set up various firewall rules about what network connections are allowed.

13.2.2 Amazon Machine Images

To start an EC2 machine, you need an operating system image. While it is possible to build custom Amazon Machine Images (AMIs), you can often use a ready-made one.

There are AMIs for all major Linux distributions. The AMI ID for the right distribution depends on the AWS *region* you want to run the machine. Once you have decided on the region and the distribution version, you need to find the AMI ID.

The ID can sometimes be non-trivial to find. If you have the *product code*, for example, aw0evgkw8e5c1q413zgy5pjce, you can use describe_images.

```
client = boto3.client('ec2', region_name='us-west-2')
description = client.describe_images(Filters=[{
    'Name': 'product-code',
    'Values': ['aw0evgkw8e5c1q413zgy5pjce']
}])
print(description)
```

The CentOS wiki contains product codes for all relevant CentOS versions.

AMI IDs for Debian images can be found on the Debian wiki. The Ubuntu website has a tool to find the AMI IDs for various Ubuntu images based on region and version. Unfortunately, there is no centralized, automated registry. It is possible to search for AMIs with the UI, but this is risky. The best way to guarantee the authenticity of the AMI is to look at the creator's website.

13.2.3 SSH Keys

For ad hoc administration and troubleshooting, it is useful to be able to SSH into the EC2 machine. This might be for manual SSH, using Paramiko, Ansible, or bootstrapping Salt.

Best practices for building AMIs, which are followed by all major distributions for their default images, use cloud-init to initialize the machine. One of the things cloud-init does is allow a preconfigured user to log in via an SSH public key retrieved from the machine's user data.

Public SSH keys are stored by region and account. There are two ways to add an SSH key; letting AWS generate a key-pair and retrieving the private key, or generating a key-pair ourselves and pushing the public key to AWS.

The first way is done as follows.

```
key = boto3.client("ec2").create_key_pair(KeyName="high-security")
fname = os.path.expanduser("~/.ssh/high-security")
```

```
with open(fname, "w") as fpout:
    os.chmod(fname, 0o600)
    fpout.write(key["KeyMaterial"])
```

There are a few things to note about this example.

- Keys are ASCII-encoded. Using string (rather than byte) functions is safe.

- It is a good idea to change the file permissions *before* putting in sensitive data.

- The ~/.ssh directory tends to have conservative permissions.

- This code only works once since key names are unique per region. To retry it, delete the keys in the console, or add some unique identifier to the key.

13.2.4 Bringing up Machines

The run_instances method on the EC2 client can start new instances. Choose IMAGE_ID based on the image you want to run by searching the console.

If you have already created any machines through the console-based wizard, you have a reasonable security group you can use for SECURITY_GROUP. Creating an initial security group that is reasonable is non-trivial. If you are new to AWS and not just to boto3, create and immediately destroy an EC2 instance through the console to get a security group.

```
client = boto3.client("ec2")
client.run_instances(
    ImageId=IMAGE_ID,
    MinCount=1,
    MaxCount=1,
    InstanceType='t2.micro',
    KeyName=ssh_key_name,
    SecurityGroupIds=[SECURITY_GROUP]
)
```

The API is a little counter-intuitive. In almost all cases, both `MinCount` and `MaxCount` need to be 1. For running several identical machines, it is much better to use an AutoScaling Group (ASG), which is beyond the scope of the current chapter. It is worth remembering that as AWS's first service, EC2 has the oldest API, with the least lessons learned on designing good cloud automation APIs.

While the API generally allows running more than one instance, this is not often done. The `SecurityGroupIds` imply which VPC the machine is in. When running a machine from the AWS console, a fairly liberal Security group is automatically created. Using this security group is a useful shortcut for debugging purposes, although it is better to create custom security groups.

The AMI chosen here is a CentOS AMI. While `KeyName` is not mandatory, it is highly recommended to create a key-pair, or import one, and use the name.

The `InstanceType` indicates the amounts of computation resources allocated to the instance. `t2.micro` is, as the name implies, a fairly minimal machine. It is useful mainly for prototyping but usually cannot support all but the most minimal production workloads.

13.2.5 Securely Logging In

When logging in via SSH, it is good to know beforehand what public key you expect. Otherwise, an intermediary can hijack the connection. Especially in cloud environments, the Trust On First Use (TOFU) approach is problematic. There are a lot of first uses whenever you create a new machine. Since VMs are best treated as disposable, the TOFU principle is of little help.

The main technique in retrieving the key is to realize that the key is written to the console as the instance boots up. AWS has a way for you to retrieve the console output.

```
client = boto3.client('ec2')
output = client.get_console_output(InstanceId=sys.argv[1])
result = output['Output']
```

Unfortunately, boot-time diagnostic messages are not well structured, so the parsing must be somewhat ad hoc.

```
rsa = next(line
           for line in result.splitlines()
           if line.startswith('ssh-rsa'))
```

Look for the first line that starts with `ssh-rsa`. Now that you have the public key, there are several things you can do with it. If you just want to run the SSH command line, and the machine is not VPN-accessible-only, you want to store the public IP in known_hosts.

This avoids a TOFU situation. `boto3` uses certificate authorities to connect securely to AWS, so the SSH key's integrity is guaranteed. Especially for cloud platforms, TOFU is a poor security model. Since it is so easy to create and destroy machines, the lifetime of machines is sometimes measured in weeks or even days.

```
resource = boto3.resource('ec2')
instance = resource.Instance(sys.argv[1])
known_hosts = (f'{instance.public_dns_name},'
               f'{instance.public_ip_address} {rsa}')
with open(os.path.expanduser('~/.ssh/known_hosts'), 'a') as fp:
    fp.write(known_hosts)
```

13.2.6 Building Images

Building your own images can be useful. One reason to do it is to accelerate start-up. Instead of booting up a vanilla Linux distribution and then installing needed packages, setting configuration, and so on, it is possible to do it once, store the AMI, and then launch instances from this AMI.

Another reason to do it is to have known upgrade times; running `apt-get update && apt-get upgrade` means getting the latest packages at the time of upgrade. Instead, doing this in an AMI build allows knowing all machines are running from the same AMI. Upgrades can be done by first replacing some machines with the new AMI, checking the status, and replacing the rest. This technique (used by Netflix, among others) is called an *immutable image*. While there are other approaches to immutability, this is one of the first successfully deployed in production.

One way to prepare machines is to use a configuration management system. Both Ansible and Salt have a local mode that runs commands locally instead of via a server/client connection.

The steps are as follows.

1. Launch an EC2 machine with the right base image (for example, vanilla CentOS).

2. Retrieve the host key for securely connecting.

3. Copy over the Salt code.

4. Copy over the Salt configuration.

5. Via SSH, run Salt on the EC2 machine.

6. At the end, call `client("ec2").create_image` to save the current disk contents as an AMI.

```
$ pex -o salt-call -c salt-call salt-ssh
$ scp -r salt-call salt-files $USER@$IP:/
$ ssh $USER@$IP /salt-call --local --file-root /salt-files
(botovenv)$ python
...
>>> client.create_image(....)
```

This approach means a simple script running on a local machine or in a CI environment can generate an AMI from source code.

13.3 Simple Storage Service (S3)

The simple storage service (S3) is an object storage service. Objects, which are byte streams, can be stored and retrieved. This can store backups, compressed log files, video files, and similar things.

S3 stores objects in *buckets* by a *key* (a string). Objects can be stored, retrieved, or deleted. However, objects cannot be modified in place.

S3 buckets names must be globally unique, not just per account. This uniqueness is often accomplished by adding the account holder's domain name; for example, `large-videos.production.example.com`.

Buckets can be set to be publicly available, in which case objects can be retrieved by accessing a URL composed of the bucket's name and the object's name. This allows S3 buckets, properly configured, to be static websites.

13.3.1 Managing Buckets

In general, bucket creation is a fairly rare operation. New buckets correspond to new code *flows*, not code *runs*. This is partially because buckets need to have unique names. However, it is sometimes useful to create buckets automatically, perhaps for many parallel test environments.

```
response = client("s3").create_bucket(
    ACL='private',
    Bucket='my.unique.name.example.com',
)
```

There are other options, but those are usually not needed. Some of those have to do with granting permissions on the bucket. In general, a better way to manage bucket permissions is how all permissions are managed by attaching policies to roles or IAM users.

In order to list possible keys, you can use the following.

```
response = client("s3").list_objects(
    Bucket=bucket,
    MaxKeys=10,
    Marker=marker,
    Prefix=prefix,
)
```

The first two arguments are important. It is necessary to specify the bucket, and it is a good idea to make sure that responses are of known maximum size.

The Prefix parameter is useful, especially when using the S3 bucket to simulate a file system. For example, this is what S3 buckets that serve as websites usually look like. When exporting CloudWatch logs to S3, it is possible to specify a prefix exactly to simulate a file system. While internally, the bucket is still flat, you can use something like Prefix="2018/12/04/" to get only the logs from December 4, 2018.

When more objects qualify than MaxKeys, the response is truncated. The IsTruncated field in the response is True, and the NextMarker field is set. Sending another list_objects with the Marker set to the returned NextMarker retrieve the next MaxKeys objects. This allows pagination through consistent responses even in the face of mutating buckets, in the limited sense that you get at least all *objects* that were not mutated while paginating.

To retrieve a single object, you use get_object.

```
response = boto3.client("s3").get_object(
    Bucket=BUCKET,
    Key=OBJECT_KEY,
)
value = response["Body"].read()
```

The value is a bytes object.

Especially for small to medium-sized objects, say up to several megabytes, this allows simple retrieval of all data.

To push such objects into the bucket, you can use the following.

```
response = boto3.client("s3").put_object(
    Bucket=BUCKET,
    Key=some_key,
    Body=b'some content',
)
```

Again, this works well for the case where the body all fits in memory.

As alluded to earlier, when uploading or downloading larger files (for example, videos or database dumps), you would like to be able to upload incrementally without keeping the whole file in memory at once.

The boto3 library exposes a high-level interface to such functionality using the *_fileobj methods. For example, you can transfer a large video file using the following.

```
client - boto3.client('s3')
with open("meeting-recording.mp4", "rb") as fpin:
    client.upload_fileobj(
        fpin,
        my_bucket,
        "meeting-recording.mp4"
    )
```

You can also use similar functionality to download a large video file.

```
client = boto3.client('s3')
with open("meeting-recording.mp4", "wb") as fpout:
    client.upload_fileobj(
```

```
    fpin,
    my_bucket,
    "meeting-recording.mp4"
 )
```

Finally, it is often the case that you would like objects to be transferred directly out of S3 or into S3 without the data going through the custom code, but you do not want to allow unauthenticated access.

For example, a continuous integration job might upload its artifacts to S3. You would like to be able to download them through the CI web interface, but having the data pass through the CI server is unpleasant. This server now needs to handle potentially larger files where people would care about transfer speeds.

S3 allows you to generate pre-signed URLs. These URLs can be given as links from another web application or sent via email or other methods and allow time-limited access to the S3 resource.

```
url = s3.generate_presigned_url(
    ClientMethod='get_object',
    Params={
        'Bucket': my_bucket,
        'Key': 'meeting-recording.avi'
    }
)
```

This URL can now be sent via email to people who need to view the recording, and they can download the video and watch it. In this case, you saved yourself any need to run a web server.

An even more interesting use case is allowing pre-signed *uploads*. This is especially interesting because uploading files sometimes requires subtle interplays between the web server and the web application server to allow large requests to be sent in.

Instead, uploading directly from the client to S3 allows you to remove all the intermediaries. For example, this is useful for some document-sharing applications.

```
post = boto3.client("s3").generate_presigned_post(
    Bucket=my_bucket,
    Key='meeting-recording.avi',
)
```

```
post_url = post["url"]
post_fields = post["fields"]
```

You can use this URL from code with something like the following.

```
with open("meeting-recording.avi", "rb"):
    requests.post(post_url,
                  post_fields,
                  files=dict(file=file_contents))
```

This lets you upload the meeting recording locally, even if the meeting recording device does not have S3 access credentials. It is also possible to limit the maximum size of the files via generate_presigned_post to prevent potential harm from an unknown device uploading these files.

Note that pre-signed URLs can be used multiple times. Making a pre-signed URL only valid for a limited time can mitigate any risk of potentially mutating the object after uploading. For example, if the duration is one second, you can avoid checking the uploaded object until the second is done.

13.4 Summary

AWS is a popular infrastructure as a service platform, which is generally used on a pay-as-you-go basis. It is suitable for automation of infrastructure management tasks, and boto3, maintained by AWS, is a powerful way to approach this automation.

CHAPTER 14

Kubernetes

Kubernetes is a popular *container orchestration framework*. It runs containers on Linux machines (virtual or physical) based on various parameters.

You can run Kubernetes (often shortened to K8s) as an open source project. Many cloud providers offer a service of managed Kubernetes, where they run Kubernetes and manage its low-level reliability.

There are two main ways that Python interacts with Kubernetes. First, Kubernetes runs Python applications. There are some important things to consider when packaging Python applications to run with Kubernetes. Second, Python can automate Kubernetes through its API.

Both are covered here.

14.1 Pods

One of the main concepts in Kubernetes is the pod. A pod is a group of containers that share a common network namespace but not a common file system. They are always run together.

Many pods (and in some Kubernetes installations, all pods) have only one container. If there is more than one container, there usually be the main container and other supporting containers, sometimes called *sidecars*. A sidecar container can do anything from terminating SSL traffic to exporting metrics and many things in between.

14.1.1 Liveness and Readiness

When configuring a pod, there are two important notions.

- Readiness
- Liveness

© Moshe Zadka 2022
M. Zadka, *DevOps in Python*, https://doi.org/10.1007/978-1-4842-7996-0_14

A *liveness* check determines whether the container needs to be restarted. If a liveness check fails, Kubernetes restarts the pod.

A Kubernetes service selects pods with criteria. Only pods where the readiness check succeeds are included in the service.

A service is often used by different methods of load-balancing traffic to decide where to send the traffic. For a service used in this way, a failed readiness check means no traffic is sent to the relevant pod. Ideally, for web-based applications, a dedicated endpoint or several endpoints is configured to determine health and readiness.

While it is possible to configure liveness checks to wait for an initial boot-up time, this is not the best way to do so.

If an application has a slow start-up time, the best way to handle it is to start responding to *liveness* early, as the application does any pre-computing or initial configuration, and configure a readiness check to indicate the initial configuration is done, and the application is ready to receive traffic.

Slow start-up is sometimes caused by needing some initial data. This data might come from a slow data service or might need slow pre-processing before being in the proper shape to respond to queries. In the following example, for simplicity, we avoid a back-end service altogether and focus on an application that requires a heavy computation before it starts.

In this toy example, a web service returns many copies of the same line: the fortieth number of the Fibonacci sequence, divided by 1000. To get a proper slow start-up, the Fibonacci sequence is implemented using the naive, slow algorithm.

```python
def fibonacci(n):
    if n < 2:
        return 1
    return fibonacci(n - 1) + fibonacci(n - 2)
```

There are faster ways to compute Fibonacci numbers. This function is useful as a stand-in for a slow computation that is harder to optimize.

To have the application be faster, there is a cache of the relevant Fibonacci numbers.

```python
fibonacci_results = {}
```

If the application starts with the following, it takes quite a while to start up.

```python
fibonacci_results[40]  =   fibonacci(40)
```

On a test machine, this took 10 to 20 seconds.

When configuring a *liveness* check, it is useful if it has a short timeout. After the application is started, something has gone seriously wrong if the liveness check takes more than a second.

However, configuring a liveness check with a 1-second timeout results in a pod that goes into a Kubernetes crash loop. This is a case where a better start-up, combined with separate readiness and liveness checks, can be useful.

The application in this example uses the `klein` web framework, which uses `Twisted` as its underlying networking framework.

The initialization logic can be deferred to a thread, and the result stored in the cache when it is available.

```
import functools, operator
from twisted.internet.threads import deferToThread

set_40 = functools.partial(operator.setitem, fibonacci_results, 40)
d = deferToThread(fibonacci, 40)
d.addCallback(set_40)
```

The code for the core business logic can be written using the cached value.

```
from klein import route

@route("/")
def fibonacci_40(request):
    stuff = fibonacci_results[40] // 1000
    return "a line\n" * stuff

from klein import run
run("localhost", 8080)
```

Notice that this code *fails* if the cache is not initialized yet. Because of this, the pod should be configured with a readiness check.

Note that while / could be configured as the readiness endpoint since it fails if the result is missing, this is suboptimal. If it does *not* fail, it does some extra computation: creating a big string and sending it to the client.

In a more realistic example, this could be even worse. For example, this might call back to a back-end service or have some undesirable side effect.

Configuring a dedicated readiness check is better.

```python
@route("/ready")
def ready(request):
    if 40 in fibonacci_results:
        return "Yes"
    raise ValueError("still initializing")
```

In this case, failure is accomplished by raising an exception. In a more sophisticated readiness code, it is sometimes worthwhile to send a specific HTTP error code and give more details. This can help in troubleshooting.

Finally, since neither of these endpoints would serve as a useful *liveness* check, the application needs a dedicated endpoint. Again, in general, it is useful to give applications dedicated health checks.

Those can do more than just serve as a way to make sure that the application's web framework is functional. They can also check configuration and connectivity, for example.

```python
@route("/health")
def healthy(request):
    return "Yes"
```

A Kubernetes pod definition for this application might have the following lines in it.

```yaml
apiVersion: v1
kind: Pod
# ...
spec:
    containers:
    - name: fibonacci
    # ...
      livenessProbe:
        httpGet:
            path: /health
            port: 8080
        periodSeconds: 3
      readinessProbe:
        httpGet:
```

```
        path: /ready
        port: 8080
    periodSeconds: 3
```

This pattern of starting up immediately but having a readiness check that stops incoming traffic is powerful. In this case, we configured a pod directly. In more realistic cases, this configuration would be part of a deployment.

Having a fast start-up and careful readiness makes blue/green deployment patterns easier to accomplish. It allows configuring which colors are active based on how many nodes are ready. Unlike `initialDelaySeconds` configured in Kubernetes, optimizations to application start-up time are immediately reflected in better use of computing resources.

Even better, *degradations* in application start-up time cause degradation in the use of computing resources, not a catastrophic failure. While the degradation should be fixed, allowing the deployment to go forward based on human decisions, not Kubernetes configuration, is an operational advantage.

14.1.2 Configuration

When writing applications that are designed to run on Kubernetes, it is important to consider where their configuration comes from. In this context, configuration refers to things that need to be different between environments (development, staging, production, etc.). Any configuration that does *not* change between the environments can be added to the container images.

Environment Variables

Environment variables are often a recommended mechanism to pass in configuration parameters. For example, this is considered the correct way in The Twelve-Factor App methodology.

Environment variables serve as a simple namespace that is accessible from anywhere in the application code and contains arbitrary data. Setting environment variables via Kubernetes is done by adding an env stanza to the container spec.

```
env:
- name: GEM_LEVEL
  value:   "diamond"
```

To access the environment variable, the application code uses the os.environ dict-like object.

```
gem_level = os.environ["GEM_LEVEL"]
```

This can be done anywhere in the application code. For the most testable code, this is best done at as high a level as possible. In web applications, this can be done where a WSGI application is constructed.

The following example uses the Pyramid web framework. With Pyramid, the code for a web application that uses the GEM_LEVEL environment variable might look as follows.

```
from pyramid import config as configlib, response

def gem_level(request):
    level = request.registry.settings["gem_level"]
    return response.Response(f"Level: {level}")

def make_app(environ):
    settings = dict(gem_level=os.environ["GEM_LEVEL"])
    with configlib.Configurator(settings=settings) as config:
        config.add_route('gem_level', '/')
        config.add_view(gem_level, route_name='gem_level')
    app = config.make_wsgi_app()
    return app
```

Note that so far, none of this code touches the os.environ dict-like object itself. It defined a make_app() function, which accepts a dict-like object as a parameter.

This makes the code easier to test without trying to patch environment variables. The top-level code creating the WSGI app would look as follows.

```
import os

application = make_app(os.environ)
```

This Python code is in a file gem_level.py.

The application object is a WSGI-compatible application. When running locally, it can be run using

```
(gem-testing) $ pip install gunicorn pyramid
(gem-testing) $ GEM_LEVEL=2 gunicorn gem_level
```

When running code locally, create and activate a virtual environment before running `pip install`.

Since gunicorn uses the `application` variable in a module by default, this code runs correctly and use the GEM_LEVEL environment variable.

The relevant Dockerfile might end with a line like the following.

```
ENTRYPOINT ["gunicorn", "gem_level"]
```

For example, for a proof-of-concept, it is possible to write a short Dockerfile.

```
FROM python
RUN pip install gunicorn pyramid
COPY gem_level.py /
ENTRYPOINT ["gunicorn", "gem_level"]
```

Note that this is not a Dockerfile suited for production use; for that, refer to Chapter 12.

Configuration Files

Kubernetes pods, and therefore, deployments, support configmap. While configmap settings can set environment variables or command-line parameters, there are different ways to set them.

One thing that configmap solves uniquely is being able to set, through the Kubernetes configuration, data that appears as a file inside a container in a pod.

This is especially useful when porting an existing Python program that already uses a configuration file to set parameters to Kubernetes. For example, gunicorn can be used to read a Paste-compatible configuration file to run a WSGI application.

For example, a Paste-based version of the Pyramid application would look as follows.

```
def make_app_ini(global_config, **settings):
    with configlib.Configurator(settings=settings) as config:
        config.add_route('gem_level', '/')
        config.add_view(gem_level, route_name='gem_level')
        app = config.make_wsgi_app()
return app
```

When using this, the line `application = make_app(os.environ)` should be removed from gem_level.py.

The following is a relevant configuration for the diamond level.

```
[app:main]
use = call:gem_level:make_app_ini

[DEFAULT]
gem_level = diamond
```

In this case, a pod configuration might be set up as follows.

```
apiVersion: v1
kind: ConfigMap
metadata:
   name: gem-level-config-diamond
data:
    paste.ini: |
        [app:main]
        use = call:gem_level:make_app_ini
        [DEFAULT]
        gem_level = diamond
--
apiVersion: v1
kind: Pod
metadata:
   name: configmap-demo-pod
spec:
   containers:
      - name: gemlevel
        image: ...
        command: ["gunicorn", "--paste", "/etc/gemlevel/paste.ini"]
        volumeMounts:
            - name: config
              mountPath: "/etc/gemlevel"
              readOnly: true
   volumes:
      - name: config
        configMap:
```

```
      name: gem-level-config-diamond
    items:
      - key: "paste.ini"
        path: "paste.ini"
```

Especially when many parameters come from the paste.ini, this can be a quicker path to moving the application to Kubernetes than moving each one to an environment variable. Note that in this case, part of the `paste.ini` was not configured as defined. The first two lines would be the same in every environment.

```
[app:main]
use = call:gem_level_ini:make_app
```

This is a common issue in moving applications when configuration files include a mix of application configuration and environment configuration.

There are ways to work around this, such as by merging configuration files. The best solution depends on the local situation and can vary.

Secrets

Secrets are similar to `configmaps`. The main difference is that if Kubernetes is set up properly, secrets are stored encrypted in the API server.

Note that this is not true by default! Setting up secret encryption in Kubernetes is a complicated topic. It often depends on the capabilities in the environment that Kubernetes is running on, whether a cloud provider or on-premises.

However, assuming secret encryption has been properly set up, this is the right place to store database passwords, API tokens, and the like.

For example, if a pod needs access to the code for a planetary defense system or the code on someone's luggage, the following configuration might work.

```
apiVersion: v1
kind: Secret
metadata:
  name: luggage
type: Opaque
data:
  code: MTIzNDU=
```

The code, in this case, is base64 encoded 12345. You can retrieve the secret from Kubernetes using

```
$ kubectl get secret luggage -o=jsonpath='{.data.code}'| base64 decode
```

In a production-grade Kubernetes deployment, secrets are protected by at-rest encryption and access controls. This command can be used when debugging local or testing Kubernetes clusters.

Kubernetes secrets can be set as files or environment variables. In general, it is best to pass them into containers as files.

Environment variables have many paths to leak accidentally or intentionally. For example, many error-reporting systems capture all environment variables to help debug.

Mounting a secret as a file is similar to mounting a configuration map.

```
spec:
  containers:
  - name: acontainer
    # ...
    env:
    - name: SECRET_CODE
      value: /etc/secrets/code
    volumeMounts:
    - name: secrets
      mountPath: "/etc/secrets"
      readOnly: true
volumes:
  - name: secrets
    secret:
    secretName: luggage
    items:
    - key: code
      path: code
```

This is a typical configuration. The application is still configured mainly via environment variables. However, the environment variable *itself* is not sensitive; it is just the literal value /etc/secrets/code. Inside the application, code might look like the following.

```
with open(os.environ["SECRET_CODE"]) as fpin:
    code = fpin.read()
```

The secret itself is only stored in the file system and the application's memory, never in an environment variable.

14.1.3 Python Sidecars

Until now, the pods in the examples were single-container pods. One of the main benefits of pods is that they can include more than one container.

All containers in a pod share a network namespace but not the filesystem. In practice, containers in a pod can be built using different stacks and different container images. They can communicate using 127.0.0.1 as an endpoint.

Containers designed to go as the other container in the pod, next to the main one, are called sidecars. It is important to note that from the perspective of Kubernetes, nothing makes a container. When managing pods, though, it is usually the case that one container does the real work while the rest are in support positions.

As a contrived example, imagine an application with a JSON diagnostic endpoint, say on /status. The HTTP status code is always 200. One of the fields in the JSON result is "database-connected": BOOLEAN, where the BOOLEAN is a JSON boolean: either true or false.

The application should not be considered ready if the database is not connected. An httpGet probe is not enough. It always returns successfully.

In a pod, all containers must be ready for the pod to receive connection. A sidecar container's readiness check can grab the main containers' status and check the database connection.

```
def readiness(request):
    result = httpx.get("http://127.0.0.1:8080").json()
    if not result["database-connected"]:
        raise ValueError("database not connected", result)
    return Response("connected")
```

```
with configlib.Configurator() as config:
    config.add_route('readiness', '/ready')
    config.add_view(readiness, route_name='readiness')
    application = config.make_wsgi_app()
```

This is a better alternative to using exec probes, which rely on running commands inside a container. Sidecars can be used for more than readiness checks: exporting metrics, proxying, scheduled cleanup, and more are just a small sample of what can be done with sidecars.

Since sidecar container images are often built ad hoc for existing images, Python is a useful language for them even if the main container is not written in Python.

14.2 REST API

Kubernetes has an OpenAPI-based RESTful API. Because the API is described using OpenAPI, clients can be automatically generated for many languages.

This has its downsides. The documentation for the Python Kubernetes client can be impenetrable at times. It is not well organized.

It is, however, explorable using a Python prompt. Describing the entire API is beyond the length of a single chapter, but it is useful to understand a few basic concepts.

The Python Kubernetes API client is installable using `pip install kubernetes`. In this package, two important modules are often imported.

The `config` module allows reading a `kubectl`-compatible configuration and connecting to the same endpoint. Since most Kubernetes management tools give such a configuration, this is useful.

The API documentation usually suggests loading a global configuration. In general, such implicit globals make code harder to understand, test, and debug.

A better approach is to use the `kubernetes.client.new_client_from_config()` function. Given no argument, this function reads the `kubectl` configuration.

If the code runs in a container run by Kubernetes, Kubernetes can have the container access a service account. If this is done, `new_client_from_config()` connects to Kubernetes as the relevant account. This allows managing Kubernetes automation and its permission directly from Kubernetes.

```
from kubernetes import config as k8config

client = k8config.new_client_from_config()
```

The kubernetes subpackages have generic names. It is often a good idea to use `import` as to make it easier to read the code that uses them.

The client returned by the function is of little use by itself. Instead, specific API areas in Kubernetes correspond to specific classes in `kubernetes.client`.

For example, the core v1 API is accessed through `kubernetes.client.CoreV1Api`. Explicitly passing the client to the code allows easier testing and centralized management of client configuration.

```
from kubernetes import client as k8client, config as k8config

client = k8config.new_client_from_config()
core = k8client.CoreV1Api(client)
```

This is the API that manages the core objects in Kubernetes: pods, namespaces, and similar low-level objects. For example, using this API, it is possible to get a list of all pods.

```
from kubernetes import client as k8client, config as k8config

client = k8config.new_client_from_config()
core = k8client.CoreV1Api(client)

res = core.list_pod_for_all_namespaces()
for pod in res.items:
    for container in pod.spec.containers:
        print(container.image)
```

This prints all container images for containers currently running in the Kubernetes installation.

14.3 Operators

Kubernetes operators are a powerful tool for customizing Kubernetes. There is only one twist: operators are not a Kubernetes concept. Instead, operators are a pattern. The pattern consists of several parts.

- One or more inputs

- One or more outputs

The operator then runs a *reconciliation loop*.

- Retrieve inputs

- Retrieve outputs

- Calculate correct inputs for the outputs

- Check the difference between the previous two steps

- Fix the differences

Fixing the differences can be done in one of two ways.

- Deleting outputs that should not exist and creating output
  that should

- Modifying incorrect output

Some things in Kubernetes cannot be modified, and only the first option is valid. Writing operators in this way tends to be easier, so this is usually the first version of an operator.

14.3.1 Permissions

Kubernetes operators need permissions to read the inputs and read/write the outputs. Since operators are regular Kubernetes API clients, they get permissions the same way all other clients get permissions: Resource-Based Access Control (RBAC).

The full details of Kubernetes RBAC are beyond the current scope. One important thing to note is that a common pattern is that operators are deployed as a Kubernetes deployment. Usually, this means the operator uses a deployment running the operators' code in pods.

These pods can be assigned a Kubernetes service role with the appropriate permissions. In this case, the API client has the right access, as long as it uses the automatically mounted API configuration to access Kubernetes.

14.3.2 Custom Types

To avoid having the inputs having any other effect, many operators also define a *custom resource type*. Kubernetes allows adding a custom type. The operator can do this, but more commonly, it is done as part of whatever process sets up the operator.

Output types may or may not be custom types; for example, if the output type is a Deployment or a ReplicaSet, it is a standard type. However, for higher-level operators, the outputs might be inputs to a lower-level operator, so a custom type.

Definining a Kubernetes custom resource type is done by creating an object of kind CustomResourceDefinition.

A useful example for the rest of the explanation is a Character type for characters from *The Wizard of Oz*. Since the story has multiple remakes, let's assign each character to a universe. Dorothy from universe 5 can only interact with characters in universe 5.

```
apiVersion: apiextensions.k8s.io/v1
kind: CustomResourceDefinition
metadata:
  name: characters.wizardofoz.example.org
spec:
  group: wizardofoz.example.org
  versions:
    - name: v1
      served: true
      storage: true
      schema:
        openAPIV3Schema:
          type: object
          properties:
            spec:
              type: object
              properties:
                name:
                  type: string
                universe:
                  type: integer
  scope: Namespaced
  names:
    plural: characters
    singular: character
    kind: Character
```

The most important part of the definition is the spec. In this case, it notes that the object has two properties: name, a string, and universe, an integer.

A Character is also created using kubectl and a YAML file.

```
apiVersion: "wizardofoz.example.org/v1"
kind: Character
metadata:
  name: a-dorothy
spec:
  name: Dorothy
  universe: 42
```

Since this is a relatively simple object, the definition is pretty short. In this case, the Character object represents Dorothy from universe 42.

Similarly, the Quest type is defined using CustomResourceDefinition.

```
apiVersion: apiextensions.k8s.io/v1
kind: CustomResourceDefinition
metadata:
  name: quests.wizardofoz.example.org
spec:
  group: wizardofoz.example.org
  versions:
    - name: v1
      served: true
      storage: true
      schema:
        openAPIV3Schema:
          type: object
          properties:
            spec:
              type: object
              properties:
                goal:
                  type: string
                universe:
                  type: integer
```

```
scope: Namespaced
names:
  plural: quests
  singular: quest
   kind: Quest
```

14.3.3 Retrieval

An operatorfirst has to get all the input objects. This is one advantage of having a custom input kind: all objects of that kind are relevant.

For non-custom types, the Kubernetes Python classes have autogenerated classes. However, for custom ones, it does not. One alternative is to regenerate the client. This is complicated and error-prone.

A quicker, though messier, an alternative is to write ad hoc classes.

Kubernetes objects have metadata. The metadata structure is consistent, so it makes sense to wrap it up in its own class.

```python
import attr
from typing import AbstractSet, Tuple

@attr.frozen
class Metadata:
    uid: str = attr.ib(eq=False)
    name: str = attr.ib(eq=False)
    namespace: str
    labels: AbstractSet[Tuple[str, str]]

    @classmethod
    def from_api(cls, result):
        return cls(
            uid=result["metadata"]["uid"],
            name=result["metadata"]["name"],
            namespace=result["metadata"]["namespace"],
            labels=frozenset(result["metadata"].get("labels", {}).items()),
        )
```

This representation of the metadata, with `frozenset` for labels and an `attr.frozen`
decorator makes `Metadata` immutable.

Immutable objects are hashable by value and can be added to sets and used as
dictionary keys. Although the operator does not require it, this is a powerful invariant in
more complicated operators.

The metadata is important to the operator: the reconciliation loop needs to match
the right input to the right output. It is also the most complicated part because, in this
case, the character and `quest` objects only have two attributes each.

```python
@attr.define
class Character:
    crd_plural = "characters"
    metadata: Metadata = attr.ib(repr=False)
    name: str
    universe: int

    @classmethod
    def from_api(cls, result):
        return cls(
            metadata=Metadata.from_api(result),
            **result["spec"],
        )


@attr.define
class Quest:
    crd_plural = "quests"
    metadata: Metadata = attr.ib(repr=False)
    goal: str
    universe: int

    @classmethod
    def from_api(cls, result):
        return cls(
            metadata=Metadata.from_api(result),
            **result["spec"],
        )
```

Putting the logical parsing code and interpreting the raw dictionary inside the object's named constructor makes the retrieval code concise and generic.

```python
from kubernetes import client as k8client

def get_custom(client, klass):
    custom = k8client.CustomObjectsApi(client)
    results = custom.list_cluster_custom_object(
        group="wizardofoz.example.org",
        version="v1",
        plural=klass.crd_plural,
    )
    for result in results["items"]:
        yield klass.from_api(result)
```

14.3.4 Goal State

After retrieving the input objects, the reconciliation loop needs to calculate the goal state: what is the right state for the output objects given the input objects.

This is the business logic of the operator. The parts until now were the plumbing: representing and getting the data from Kubernetes.

The code here is based on the book *The Wizard of Oz*.

- Dorothy wants to go home.
- The Scarecrow wants a brain.
- The Tin Man wants a heart.
- The Cowardly Lion wants courage.

Other characters in this journey-style story are encountered, but none have a quest. When the operator encounters a different character, such as Glinda, it does not create a quest for it.

```python
import uuid

def quests_from_characters(characters):
    name_to_goal = dict(
        Dorothy="Going home",
        Scarecrow="Brain",
```

```
        Tinman="Heart",
        Lion="Courage",
    )
    for character in characters:
        name = character.name
        try:
            goal = name_to_goal[name]
        except KeyError:
            continue
        quest = Quest(
            Metadata(
                uid="",
                name=str(uuid.uuid4()),
                labels=frozenset([("character-name", character.metadata.
                name)]),
                namespace=character.metadata.namespace,
            ),
            goal=goal,
            universe=character.universe,
        )
        yield quest
```

Note that the name is automatically generated as a UUID. This is useful since it guarantees there are no collisions with little effort. Many Kubernetes loops, including built-in loops like Deployment and ReplicaSet, include a UUID-like name.

14.3.5 Comparison

This representation of the goal state as a generator of quests is not the most convenient. The easiest way to compare the existing quests to the goal quests is to match them to the original character.

```
def by_character(quests):
    ret_value = {
        dict(quest.metadata.labels).get("character-name"):  quest
```

```
    for quest in quests
}
if None in ret_value:
    del ret_value[None]
return ret_value
```

A quest not marked with a `character-name` label is assumed to have been manually added. The operator leaves such quests alone. In a more realistic example, one of the labels added would have been to note the quest as created by the operator, and those not created by the operator would have been filtered out.

After conveniently representing the data, the operator *compares* the goal state with the existing state.

```
import enum

@enum.unique
class Action(enum.Enum):
    delete = enum.auto()
    create = enum.auto()

def compare(*, existing, goal):
    for character, quest in goal.items():
        try:
            current_quest = existing[character]
        except KeyError:
            pass
        else:
            if current_quest == quest:
                continue
            yield Action.delete, current_quest
        yield Action.create, quest
    for character, current_quest in existing.items():
        if character in goal:
            continue
        yield Action.delete, current_quest
```

The comparison generates an `Action.delete` result for any quest that exists and should not and an `Action.create` result for any quest that does exist and should. Some operators instead choose to disable invalid goals and delete them later as part of a garbage collection process. This can be useful for troubleshooting operators.

14.3.6 Reconciliation

To reconcile the desired state with the existing state, the actions need to be performed by the Kubernetes API client. There are two options: using the `CustomObjectsApi` or using `DynamicClient`.

The `DynamicClient` requires a more upfront setup, though it leads to simpler code for creating objects. Since this is a simple operator, the overhead of an upfront setup is more than its worth.

The reconciliation code in this operator uses `CustomObjectsApi` to delete and create objects.

```python
def perform_actions(actions):
    custom = k8client.CustomObjectsApi(client)
    for kind, details in actions:
        if kind == Action.delete:
            custom.delete_namespaced_custom_object(
                "wizardofoz.example.org",
                "v1",
                "default",
                "quests",
                details.metadata.name,
            )
        elif kind == Action.create:
            body = dict(
                apiVersion="wizardofoz.example.org/v1",
                kind="Quest",
                metadata=dict(
                    name=details.metadata.name,
                    labels=dict(details.metadata.labels)
                ),
```

```
            spec=dict(goal=details.goal, universe=details.universe),
        )
    custom.create_namespaced_custom_object(
        "wizardofoz.example.org",
        "v1",
        "default",
        "quests",
        body
    )
```

Note that with the CustomObjectsApi the creation logic has to duplicate some parameters between the body and the call to create_namespaced_custom_object().

14.3.7 Combining the Pieces

Now that all the pieces are in place, the reconcile() function takes a preconfigured client objects and puts those pieces together to get the data and generate the reconciliation API calls.

```
def reconcile(client):
    goal_quests = by_character(
        quests_from_characters(get_custom(client, Character))
    )
    existing_quests = by_character(get_custom(client, Quest))
    actions = compare(existing=existing_quests, goal=goal_quests)
     perform_actions(actions)
```

Finally, running the code depends on how the operator is configured. In the following example, the assumption is that the default configuration is enough. If this is not the case, it might make sense to pass configuration more explicitly.

```
from kubernetes import config as k8config
import time

client = k8config.new_client_from_config()
while True:
    reconcile(client)
    time.sleep(30)
```

It is possible to avoid polls by using the `watch()` API, which makes the code slightly more complicated. In practice, polling loops have little enough overhead. They are easier to write and troubleshoot, so it is usually a good idea to avoid the `watch()` API until it has proven necessary.

14.4 Summary

Kubernetes is a popular choice for container orchestration. In practice, it ends up running many Python-based containerized applications. Understanding the capabilities it offers allows building containers that take advantage of those capabilities.

Automating Kubernetes is possible through its API. This API allows retrieving and manipulating data. This can be used in CI/CD systems to trigger deployment and troubleshoot scripts to quickly find issues.

One kind of automation is called the *operator pattern*, which is a reconciliation loop creating, deleting, or modifying Kubernetes API objects based on different objects. In a more general sense, either the operator's inputs or outputs can be external. For example, an operator can be triggered by the existence of a row in a database or might update values in a web service.

Python is well-suited to writing ad hoc, local operators. Those can harmonize the way the Kubernetes cluster is set up, avoiding the need to synchronize tooling and configuration in a separate place from the cluster, such as a chart or template repository.

CHAPTER 15

Terraform

Terraform is an open source project maintained by HashiCorp, which gives an infrastructure as code (IaC) interface to cloud providers.

The idea behind IaC is that instead of managing cloud infrastructure via the console UI or explicitly calling create/delete/update APIs. The code describes the *desired* state of affairs.

The system (in this case, Terraform) is responsible for reconciling the actual cloud infrastructure with the desired state. This means that the infrastructure is *managed* as code; updates to the infrastructure are code reviewed, approved, and then merged.

Terraform is a powerful and sophisticated project. There are many resources to learn how to use it, such as the official tutorial on `terraform.io` or many video tutorials on YouTube.

Terraform's native language, HCL, is a domain-specific language to define infrastructure configuration. In more sophisticated use-cases, it is easy to run to its limit.

For example, HCL does have a for-like construct for creating several similar objects that are different by a parameter. It lacks, however, a *conditional* statement.

This means that while it is possible to create several AWS S3 buckets, it is not possible to set or not set a time-to-live (TTL) on the objects in them based on a parameter. In this example, it is possible to set a long TTL on the objects.

These workarounds and accommodations stack up quickly and complicate the HCL sources with comments explaining why each was necessary. For cases like this, it is possible to programmatically generate Terraform configurations.

One way to generate Terraform configurations is using the native Cloud Development Kit (CDK), which supports several languages, among them Python. At the time of writing, the CDK and `cdktf` tools are still in beta.

A different approach is to take advantage of a lesser-known feature of Terraform. Terraform can take its input not just in HCL but also in JSON. Any programming language, including Python, can generate these JSON files.

225

© Moshe Zadka 2022
M. Zadka, *DevOps in Python*, https://doi.org/10.1007/978-1-4842-7996-0_15

Terraform is used to configure cloud environments, and learning to use it properly takes time and practice. The following examples do not focus on teaching Terraform but on how to *automate Terraform configuration* using Python. Because of this, the examples contain a Terraform usage that is much simpler than configuring cloud environments.

Terraform contains the local provider, which allows reading and writing local files. This is not a good use case for Terraform but a great source of examples for automating Terraform configuration.

The following examples create Terraform configurations that produce a directory with files containing greetings for someone. In a more realistic Terraform usage, the files are stand-ins for some cloud-based resource, like an AWS S3 bucket or a Google GKS cluster.

The examples also contain the name of the person being greeted. This is a stand-in for the things which differ between different environments. The same Terraform configuration is used to create the staging and production clusters.

15.1 JSON Syntax

The native Terraform HCL is more convenient for writing Terraform configuration by hand. Before learning how to generate JSON configurations automatically, it is useful to learn how to write them by hand, even if this is not convenient.

Usually, the provider configuration—often put in a `main.tf` file—does not need to be generated since it tends to be constant across environments.

The main things that need to be configured are Terraform resources and Terraform variables. Unlike in HCL, when using JSON, each resource or variable needs to be in its own file. While this makes it harder to write by hand, it makes it somewhat easier to generate.

Terraform requires a provider to make changes. Most providers are real cloud providers. In these examples, the local provider is used. Configuring a local provider does not require any parameters. Providers arc usually configured in a file called `main.tf`.

```
terraform {
    required_providers {
        local = {
            source  =     "hashicorp/local"
            version =  "2.1.0"
        }
```

```
    }
}
provider "local" {
}
```

The following example writes a greeting into a file. The person being greeted is configured with a variable.

This is a `person.tf.json` file.

```
{
    "variable": {
        "person": {
            "default": "Person"
        }
    }
}
```

The following is a `greeting.tf.json` file.

```
{
    "resource": {
        "local_file": {
            "simple": {
                "content": "hello ${var.person}\n",
                "filename": "${path.module}/sandbox/greeting"
            }
        }
    }
}
```

Run Terraform to create the greeting.

```
$ terraform init
...
$ TF_VAR_person=me terraform apply -auto-approve
...
$ cat sandbox/greeting
hello me
```

15.2 Generating Terraform Configurations

In the previous example, there was only one greeting: *hello*. If you need several greetings, some of them working slightly differently, it makes sense to *generate* the Terraform `.tf.json` files from code.

The code can have the relevant parameters baked into it if it makes sense or accepts them from some configuration source if the same code might need to generate different configurations. It is useful, in general, to use the native Terraform parametrizing abilities to create different *environments* while using the generators to create different objects in the same environment that still share some commonalities. The person variable is kept as a Terraform-level variable and not generated from the code.

The first step in generating a `local_file` resource, equivalent to the earlier resource written by hand, is to *generate* the right shape for the data structure.

The `resource_from_content` function gets content and an index, and it makes sure the `greeting-<index>` file has that content.

```
def resource_from_content_idx(content, idx):
    filename = "${path.module}/sandbox/greeting-" + str(idx)
    resource = dict(resource=dict(
        local_file={
            f"greeting_{idx}": dict(
                filename=filename,
                content=content,
            )
        }
    ))
    return resource
```

This function is fairly generic. It does not really understand greetings. It is focused on the shape of the Terraform resource, which is often a useful abstraction. The more sophisticated the generator is, the more it makes sense to refactor abstractions like this into a Terraform generator utility library.

At some point, the generator does need to have a specific code. In this example, farewell greetings add a see you later. Silly as it sounds, this is a stand-in for a typical use case. Often, the different objects generated might have some conditional parts. This tends to be the simplest case where a generator is useful.

The HCL language can make simple loops. It does not have a loop-with-conditional, which is often the first case where the limitations become apparent, and moving to a configuration generator makes sense.

```
def content_from_greeting(greeting):
    content = greeting + " ${var.person}"
    if greeting.endswith("bye"):
        content += ", see you later!"
    content += "\n"
    return content
```

Putting these two functions together gives something that generates JSON-able objects from a series of greetings.

```
def resources_from_greetings(all_greetings):
    for idx, greeting in enumerate(all_greetings):
        content = content_from_greeting(greeting)
        resource = resource_from_content_idx(content, idx)
        yield resource
```

Using yield allows returning an iterator over the objects. Often, these tend to be a better abstraction than something that needs to explicitly call the function once at a time since they can maintain a local state. In this case, the state is the index, making sure the files do not collide.

Finally, the files need to be written with the write JSON contents. In the following example, the built-in enumerate() is used again. Note that the names of the actual files into which the resources are written are not important. Terraform does not care about the file names, only the contents.

```
import json

resources = resources_from_greetings(["hello", "hi", "goodbye", "bye"])
for idx, resource in enumerate(resources):
    with open(f"greeting-{idx}.tf.json", "w") as fpout:
    fpout.write(json.dumps(resource))
```

After generating, Terraform needs to be run. Running Terraform post-generation depends on how the rest of the flow needs to be done. If this is done in a persistent directory, terraform init does not need to be re-run every time. If something like

Terraform Cloud is used, after generation, you can use the TF Cloud API to upload the .tf.json files (along with any manually maintained .tf files) instead of having TF Cloud track your repository.

In the simple case here, as a demonstration, after running the generator, you can apply the configuration immediately.

```
$ terraform init
$ TF_VAR_person=me terraform apply -auto-approve
```

This creates all greeting files under a sandbox, with the farewell greetings having an additional "see you later."

15.3 Summary

cdktf may become a reliable, production-grade tool in the future. It is not reliable enough to be the basis of an infrastructure as code pipeline.

Since Terraform can natively process configuration in JSON, a file format that can be reliably generated from Python, one way to automate Terraform is to generate such JSON files and then run Terraform plan/apply the usual way. This is better than using various text templating languages to generate HCL because it removes two unnecessary steps that reduce reliability and increase complexity.

- Text templating languages are often limited themselves and extensible with Python. Directly using Python removes one step of indirection.

- Text templating language does not understand HCL and can result in invalid HCL. When writing JSON, the JSON output is always valid JSON. Higher-level abstractions in Python can guarantee that higher-level syntax will be correct.

This mechanism is fully compatible with anything in the Terraform ecosystem since this ecosystem is already set up for integration with Terraform JSON configuration. Whether you run Terraform manually from a console, automatically from a CI, use Terraform Cloud, or Terraform Enterprise, this is compatible with all workflows. It is also compatible with separating the planning and execution phases and using a pre-written plan.

Index

© Moshe Zadka 2022
M. Zadka, *DevOps in Python*, https://doi.org/10.1007/978-1-4842-7996-0

Printed in the United States
by Baker & Taylor Publisher Services